As a Christian myself, I felt this r

a lively story of her life with Christ. Her insight and her Faith is an eye opener for dedication to the Lord God. May our Faith reach to others as hers' has.

- Margaret Brown,

Secretary

This book is a beautiful masterpiece. It is so heartfelt and real. I think it will really touch others in this world after they read it. I am so happy she wrote it for others to enjoy. I think it is a real treasure. I loved reading it and couldn't put it down. She has such great faith and commitment that it makes me want to do more for the Lord.

- Donna Thompson, Retired

High School Teacher

As I read Beth Springer's book, I was made aware of the Father's love on a greater level. I was also challenged to live for Him more and more every day. Beth's relationship with the Lord, as expressed in her book, captivates the heart and the mind and draws you into a greater level of desire for the Lord.

- Rev. V. Justin Smith,

Christian Life Church

Thank you for sharing your life journey with me. It was very powerful, Uplifting, and inspiring to me. The book is a must read!

- Shelly Lindstrom

This book was written from the heart of a woman who is truly a King's daughter. Beth's openness and transparency reveals her deep love for her God. I was blessed and encouraged as I read her inspiring story and life experiences.

- Rebecca Brown, Wife of Pastor Steve Brown,
the Author of the Forgiveness section of this book

I believe this book will show those who are searching what God can do and how he can use us and answer our prayers. I personally know Beth and Barry through our Church, Christian Life and have witnessed some of this journey with them.

- Coretta Williams,
Physician Administrative
Office Assistant, Palmetto Health

Beth Springer's story is one of hope and encouragement. She is an example of someone who lives her faith out loud. Her walk with the Lord is very evident throughout this story as is the evidence of His impact on her life. This book will help the reader to become more grounded in their own faith and grow in boldness for growing the Kingdom of God.

- Cynthia Timm

Blessings! This book is worthy of obedience and the commitment it took in the authoring process of sharing how God worked in her life and in his own way to reveal her obedience and submission, to obey his word in such a personal way to share this experience, and opening doors for others to flourish and submit obedience to God. It is a privilege to share this walk through her witness and sharing. I know Beth in this role of author from a personal standpoint of living.

- Dr. Elizabeth Holmes, Educator, Administrator;
for Elementary and College, Teacher Workshops,
and Sunday School Teacher.

What a blessing this book will be to all of Beth and Barry's children, grand-children, and great-grandchildren. They will be able to have a written record of a story of faith and a great relationship to the great God of the universe- Father, Son, and Holy Spirit. My prayer is that they will appreciate all the time Beth has put into her story and have a real desire to follow in her footsteps. This book represents many hours of work in getting down on paper- blessings to you, Beth! And may this legacy for your descendants be highly valued.

- Tina McLeod

I am honored that Beth asked me to read/proof her book before it is published and to write an endorsement. I met Beth thru my father-in-law, Barry Tucker. I would like to say that her FAITH in God has inspired me to be a better Christian and I hope and pray that one day my faith is as strong as hers. To read her story is a great inspiration and I know that with her in my life that she will help me be a stronger person and to walk with God, our Savior, as well she will help many who do not know God to become acquainted with Him through this book or if you ever get the pleasure to meet her she will inspire you to be Christian.

Trust in the Lord with all your heart and lean not on your own understanding. In all your ways acknowledge Him, and he will make your paths straight. Proverbs 3:5-6

- Beth Tucker

With Love,
God Bless You,
Beth Springer

My Life with Jesus and Butterflies

My Life with Jesus and Butterflies

Beth Springer

Xulon Elite

Xulon Press Elite
2301 Lucien Way #415
Maitland, FL 32751
407.339.4217
www.xulonpress.com

Printed in the United States of America.

ISBN-13: 9781545625415

Dedication

I DEDICATE THIS BOOK TO MY MOM, DAITHY COLLINS, to my sister, Donna Thompson, my husband, Barry Tucker, Rosetta Egot, a friend in Christ, Margaret Brown, a close friend who is deep in my Lord Jesus, my Awesome Sunday School teacher, Reverend Steve Brown, and Elizabeth Holmes, a friend who is an educator, as I am, and a deep spiritual woman.

My mom has been a beacon of truth in helping me believe in my Jesus. She helps me by calling me every day to check on me and my Barry. She is a deep faithful Christian who walks and talks the faith. She is a deep mentor to me and I treasure the time I spend with her. My sister has been there to help me with my hurt husbands, and to be a help when I need someone to talk with, and be a beacon of hope when I need it. She is my best friend in this world and is a beautiful woman of Christ. My husband, Barry has helped me become more generous when I cross the path of a needy person. He has also helped me love others no matter who they are. He is a very Caring and Generous person. My friend Rosetta has a smile on her face and just reminds me of a soul that loves My Jesus so deeply. She is a beautiful person in the Lord and she walks with my Savior every day. My friend Margaret is a mentor to me and she is deep in the Lord. She is on fire for my Lord and she is like me that she reaches out to the lost and has Jesus to guide her. She has a deep love for others and it shows in her life. My Sunday School Teacher,

Reverend Steve Brown, has been a help with many facets of my faith. He is an excellent teacher and knows how to get the word into us with mature thinking. He is the author of the Forgiveness Lessons chapter in this book. He teaches us out of his heart, and we gain a wealth of knowledge in God's word. Thank you for your loving care and deep heart for our Lord, Mr. Steve Brown. Mrs. Elizabeth is a mentor who loves children just as I do, and she lives for My Savior every day of her life. She is a wonderful child of God and has a beautiful voice for our Lord. She has a heart of Gold for the needy and the unsaved. She loves My Jesus with a sweet heart and loving kindness. I wish I had known her when I taught school. She truly is one of God's saints.

TABLE OF CONTENTS

FOR THIS REASON, I KNEEL BEFORE THE FATHER, FROM whom his whole family in Heaven and on earth derives its name, I pray that out of his glorious riches He may strengthen you with power through His spirit in your inner being, so that Christ may dwell in your hearts through Faith. I pray that you be rooted in love, may have power, together with all the saints, to grasp how wide and deep is the love of Christ, to know this love that surpasseth knowledge-that you may be filled to the measure of all the fullness of God. Now to him who is able to do immeasurably more than all we ask or imagine according to his power that is at work within us, to be Glory in the church and in Christ Jesus throughout all generations forever and ever! Amen (Ephesians 3:14-20)

INTRODUCTION

I AM A FIRST- GRADE TEACHER OF 36 YEARS AND I AM retired today as we speak. I would like to share with you my walk with my Lord Jesus. It has been an awesome time in my life with Him as ruler. I gave my life to Him over 30 years ago. You can have this walk if you desire with all your heart and soul to make Him ruler of your life. He becomes REAL when you hunger and thirst for Him. He will talk with you and walk with you if you give Him control of your life. That is the key to obtaining a deep walk with Him. Just ask Jesus to come into your life and ask Him to forgive your sins, all of them, and believe that He rose from the dead and reigns on high. Draw close to Him and he will draw close to you. Also love Him with all your heart, soul, spirit, and mind. Daily talk to Him and become a friend to Him. He is just waiting for your response. Read His word and make it a light unto your path and He will actually talk to you through His word. Pray and He will hear you and answer your requests and help you in your decisions. He will open paths for you to follow and close other ones that lead to destruction. This is easy and He loves you and He wants you to come to know Him. He does not want any to perish. I am a simple woman that hungered and thirsted after my Lord. This is to show you that God can work in your life like He has done in this simple woman's life. I am not a preacher or a missionary but a common everyday person that the Lord Jesus became alive in my life and He can in yours as well. God does not just pick and choose. He wants to be a part of every person's life and it would really thrill Him to have you become His child and walk with Him in love and devotion. Give it a try and you will see how much he loves you.

My early life without my Lord Jesus

I will begin my testimony with how I met him (Jesus) and he became real to me. I grew up in a home with a brother and a sister and my dad and mom. My mom took us to a Baptist church and dad did not go. I did not get the training I needed to understand the gospel. I, in a child's mind said, "I did not kill him and therefore I am not guilty." I held on to this stupid knowledge and found no desire to serve or know my Savior. I never felt like I needed God in my life. He was not important to me and I never prayed to him or ever cared to be in his company. The Lord never was taught to me as a child so I could ask questions and get closer to him. That never happened and oh, how I wish it had happened. I was taken with teaching and my heart never felt that I needed to know God. I was blind and did not know it. I grew up and was accepted to a teacher college in the upstate, and I wanted to become a teacher. I had a dream of meeting a man at the lake. In the dream, I was walking down a hill towards a lake with 2 islands in the background and a guy with dark hair was standing between me and the lake. This dream did happen because I met Lee at the Lake with 2 islands in the background. He taught me how to water ski in that lake a few weeks after I had this dream. I went to Winthrop College to become a teacher. I had taught my baby dolls and I had a desire to teach little children. Just before I went to college I met my Lee at Lake Murray (in the dream) and we started dating and we dated throughout the 3 years I attended college. He would drive up to Rock Hill to see me and we became engaged within 3 months of dating. I did not know my Jesus at this time. I felt that I was as happy as I could be by having a wonderful boyfriend and profession. I married Lee when I finished college.

MY Wedding picture to Lee 1974

Lee was a wonderful husband and I loved him and he loved me. Our marriage lasted almost 33 years. He died one month short of our 33rd Anniversary. The very first time I encountered the Lord Jesus was at Lee's dad's funeral a few months after we were married in '74. Lee's father was a Pastor and he had a heart attack on the pulpit of his church preaching to the people. He died in the church and Lee and I attended his funeral. We were sitting on the front row and I felt a presence, not of this world. I asked Lee if he felt a presence in the church. He said that he felt nothing. I told him I felt a presence that was full of love, a love that is not like any on earth. It was deeper and sweeter than the love he had for me. More sweeter and deeper love than my mom and dad or any other person on earth. My mom years later told me that she had felt the same thing I had felt and she looked for a deeper church whereby she might encounter this LOVE that she had experienced at Lee's father's funeral.

The next few years I taught 1st grade and loved teaching. I would cry when the children left for the summer because I loved it so much. My husband, Lee ventured out to start a business that he wanted to do. He stayed in this business for the rest of his life. He was a trim carpenter and he trimmed houses for his work. I after 5 years teaching decided to pursue my Master's degree to help me teach all the children with different methods of learning, to be able to be an effective teacher for every child. I loved learning about how to reach my little guys that found learning wasn't as easy as it is to a lot of children. I valued all children I taught. Every child I wanted to be able to teach and reach no matter what I needed to do to teach them tactilely or visually. Children learn in different ways and I wanted to reach them all and be successful. I know today that God made me want to teach and gave me the desire to teach these sweet angels.

5

My first Year Teaching my 1ˢᵗ graders. 1977

One weekend Lee and I went to the mountains with my mom and dad. They were fireballs for the Lord. We were camping out of our van that was customized with a bed and kitchen. Mom and dad were camping out of their customized van also. We cooked out on stoves that were under tents. We ate supper and then went down some water slides in the mountains. We had fun. When we returned from the outing I became very sick. I stayed in the campground's bathroom. I finally thought I felt better and I returned to the van because it was getting late at night. I climbed in with Lee and tried to sleep. All of a sudden, I asked Lee to help me get to the restroom. He stood me up beside the van and let go of me to close the sliding door. I fell to the ground and my eyes rolled back into my head. Lee was afraid I was in a bad place. He carried me up to the restroom and then went to get my dad. I was out cold on the floor of the restroom. My dad laid his hands on me and prayed for my healing. I came to and felt pins and needles going through my limbs and feeling was returning to my body. Dad prayed me back to life. I do not know where I was when I was out cold. I know one thing that my dad's faith restored me back to life. I hugged my dad and thanked him for his prayers. They were powerful prayers. I had food poisoning and for a 115 pound woman it took a lot out of me. After this event, Lee said I could have died and left him childless. We started thinking about having children. Lee built our beautiful house that sits on 10.68 acres of land. We loved each other and decided to wait on children until we got the home and my Master's degree finished which stretched to 10 years. We paid for our home with cash money and Lee's labor and friends and family helping as well. Our home never had a mortgage because those ten years we saved and paid cash to build it. We made our home special by putting cypress wood in the Living room. We took beams and vaulted the master bedroom ceiling and made a balcony and beautiful plate glass up on the 2nd story. You have to climb the ladder to see out of the plate glass windows on the second floor. It seems to be the biggest room in the house because of the vaulted ceiling. Lee built this house out of love for me and I helped him as much as I could. Our home was the only home he ever built from the ground up and the last one he used with a hammer. The homes he worked in after our house were built by nail guns. He was a very talented and wonderful husband in every way. We always planned our life together and never spoke of that word so many speak of today….divorce .

Our first child was born to us just as we were finishing the house. She was a beautiful girl. I was in labor and ran a high fever and kept it till the baby was born. Naturally, the doctor thought I had an infection because of the fever, and he was going to treat the infection and send me home until they found out I was dilated and ready to have the baby. I had my children natu-rally…no drugs. The doctor almost didn't catch the baby because of my fever. Later he visited me in my room and said he had never seen a woman have a baby with fever. He said I was rare. Two years later we have our second child who was a beautiful boy. Again, I ran fever and the doctor was ready to send me home for an infection and I was two weeks over due. My mom alerted the doctor to the information that I had run fever with the first child and he decided to check me for dilation and found I was ready to deliver the baby. He almost didn't catch the baby. Again, this doctor told me he had never seen a woman deliver a baby with fever. This was a different doctor than the one I had before for the first child. He said it was extremely rare and he had never seen fever with a woman in labor. God made me this way.

Me 1980

My Life Beginning with my Lord Jesus

Now, I began my life with my God. My grand-mother was living in my home and taking care of the babies and cooking and cleaning. She was a joy to Lee and I, and she loved the children and took excellent care of them. She lived about 45 minutes away and she would go home on Fridays when I got home from teaching. Then on Sunday she would return to the house and live with us till Friday. We enjoyed her so much and this went on for years. Sometimes she had to go to court or meet the doctor, and I had to have alternative care for about one day. So, I went to check out the daycares in my community. The first one I visited I walked in and they blew a whistle and the children scampered like squirrels to the corners of the room. I was upset and walked back out. They were treating children like animals. I went to another day care and I walked in and saw all the babies in the middle of the floor with no clothes on. I was hurt to see the way they treated the babies. I was getting very upset by what I witnessed in these daycares. I went to the third daycare and I walked in and the room was dark and a tv was playing and all the kids were around the tv. I again said I would not trust my kids there for anything. I was very distraught and I knew that I had it made in the shade with my grandmother. I finally put them in a church daycare for one day and they contracted pink eye and an ear infection. My grandmother was an angel from the Lord except I did not realize it until later. One Friday night my grandmother went home, and I received a phone call from my mom (grandmother is my mom's mom). She told me that my grandmother was very sick and might die if she did not go to the hospital. I said put her on the phone. I told her I had a bad dream and my house was on fire. Fire dreams mean death. The dream was Lee sitting on the ridge of our house putting out a little fire flaming up on the ridge. He had a hose and was putting it out. I told her that Lee was not sick and neither were the kids. I wasn't sick and that left you, grandmother. Please go to the Orangeburg Hospital because you might die. Let me explain to you, the reader, about Fire dreams. Whenever I, or mom, or my sister has a fire dream it means someone will die or come very close to dying. The Lord sends these to us as a warning. I will wake up and ask what does that mean. I wake up and really get to praying because of the meaning of the dream. If it occurs on a house it means that someone in that house is in danger of dying. So, when my grandmother was so sick and might die I asked her to go to the hospital because of my fire dream. She lived most of the week with us. Mom called back and said she was going. In the meantime, I go in my guest room of my house kneeled and said, "I do not know you, but I want to ask you one request. If I take my kids to church, will you spare my grandmother's life and allow her to keep my children until they both get in school? Like I said I do not know you, Lord. I am bargaining with you to spare her life. Please honor my request." Then Lee and I and the children took off to the hospital that was an hour away. When we arrived, my mom said that my grandmother had died and they were shocking her back to life. They shocked her one time, no response. They shocked her a second time, no response. They shocked her a third time and she revived and came back to life. She lived until my son got into kindergarten. She kept our children for a few more years after this incident. God honored my request and she lived like I had asked him. I took my kids to a Baptist Church 5 minutes from the house. I had to sit with my son (2) in the class he was in and I honored my bargain with the Lord. A few weeks before this incident I sat on the steps of my house and said," I am not happy. I have everything that you can have in your life to be happy. I have beautiful children, beautiful husband, wonderful home, a reliable vehicle, and a job I adore teaching first graders. Why am I not happy? I should be happy. I have everything that is supposed to make a person happy."

Lee, Mom, My grandmother, my daughter, my son, and me 1990

Well I kept taking the kids to church and eventually I was able to attend a grownup class. I started to get hungry for My God. I had seen how he answered to the letter everything I asked for with my grandmother. One day in this church the pastor asked us in the Church if we had done anything for him that week. Had we talked and shared Jesus. Had we prayed and sought out the Lord one time that week. Had we read our bibles. I asked myself if I had and I said I had no time. I was too busy. I said to myself that needs to change. So, I tried reading the bible late at night. I fell asleep with the bible in my hand. So, I said I need to pray. I started talking to God like I do a perfect friend on my way to school in my vehicle. I started getting up 15 minutes before the family got up to go and get ready for the day. That is when I read my bible each morning before my family got up. I read 15 minutes each day and it took me over 2 years to read all of the bible. My music started changing from rock to Christian. My magazines they became Christian. My favorite magazine is the Charisma magazine. I started wearing a cross and I started singing to my God with my cassette tape machine. Many things on the TV would make me cringe. I would change the channel and monitor the words and the things they said. GD would get the TV turned off. If Lee was watching and GD was spoken I left the room. I went up every Sunday to dedicate my life to the Lord. I wasn't sure I was saved. I was hungering for my God and I wanted to know him.

Me in love with the Lord Jesus 1991

Meeting my Lord on the Beach and my Life After His Visit

So, on October 30, 1992, I took my mom, grandmother, and 2 children to the beach. We had a house right on the front beach. We went out to be on the Beach and took chairs to sit. My children were very small and played in the sand and made sandcastles. The children got tired and mom and grandmother went back to the house and left me on the beach with my cassette player singing to My God. This is the first time I heard His voice. He said, "Stand up. I bring you the peace that surpasseth understanding." Thousands of butterflies descended on the beach in a tunnel formation that spiraled down and I danced with the butterflies and screamed, "You are real". I was so thrilled to see butterflies in Oct. when there are none in SC on such a bleak and gray day. Later that day, we are on the front beach again and my daughter writes in the sand, DO YOU KNOW JESUS? He will save you from your sins. Some ladies were walking on the beach and asked me "Who wrote that?" I said, "That little girl over there." They said," Wow, she is an angel from the Lord." I said, "Thank you she is". When the waves came in and washed away the words in their place were shark's teeth and I mean in abundance. Those teeth were big and so beautiful. God blessed my daughter with beautiful artifacts from the beach.

The Beach where I met the butterflies and my God 1992

A few days later I was in a Sunday school class of the Baptist Church with my teacher and I asked the question, "Once saved Always saved." I asked them to produce the scripture that supports that idea. The next Sunday they could not show me in scripture where it was. I soon starting looking for a deeper walk with my God. So, in the paper there was a theatrical program around Easter that was being put on by a church in West Columbia. The program depicted the birth, life, and death of Jesus on the stage. The play was masterfully magnificent in the way they honored him as their Savior. So, I got some tickets to go to the program and it was life changing. The people were looking up at Heaven with their hands raised to Heaven and with all their souls were praising my God with all of their being. I decided to go to that church the next morning and visit. I got hungry and went after my need for My God.

Upon going to this Church, I was offered something I had never heard of before. They offered me the Baptism of the Holy Spirit. I wanted it because these folks were on fire for the Lord, and I wanted it too. I went up and had myself prayed over for this Holy Spirit and my little son followed me and he came away speaking in another language. A few weeks later, I felt a Holy breath breathe down my neck in this church; I received the Holy Spirit and came alive in my walk with the Lord Jesus. Wow, I found power in my prayers over others. In the next part of my story I will tell you about all the wonderful things my Lord has done in my life. Some are amazing and cannot be explained away. God will empower you with his Spirit. I know because I found this to be true in my life. I pray that everyone who reads this book will chase after my God as I did.

Now I will tell you about a sin I committed while indwelt with this Holy Spirit. I flagrantly committed a sin and knew it was against the commandments and when I arrived home and sat on my couch. I, then began to hear a crying and sobbing person inside me and I felt terrible and promised never ever will I grieve the Holy Spirit again. I actually sobbed and wept with him, and I was so sorry. I asked for forgiveness and knew that I had to be careful and never grieve Him again. So far, I have tried to keep sin out of my life and He has never sobbed again. I do have times that I have to ask forgiveness for times I let Him down, but I try to be holy and pure in his sight. He knows that we love him and look to live for Him without all that sin in our lives. We live to please him because He loves us deeply like a father.

In the meantime, while I am chasing after my God my Lee is not. He doesn't believe in God and he calls me loony tunes because I go to church with my children. He blames God for the terrible time he had with his stepmother.

She abused him and he could not understand how a loving God would allow such abuse and not do something about it. I told him that he is blaming the wrong person. Lee's mother had died when he was only 3 years old and he never remembered her. His dad brought that stepmother into his life. His dad is to blame. Our God did not have a hand in that decision. I never could bring him into that understanding. So, I hid my wonderful life in the Lord from him. I loved him and prayed for him with all my soul and body because I did not want him to go to that terrible awful place called Hell.

When I was unsaved I had a recurring dream of falling into a tunnel and never hitting bottom. It was a dream that scared me and made me uneasy. I did not understand it. I knew it meant something but it never crossed my mind that I was LOST. But I was and I would soon quit having that dream. I have never had it since I got saved. Hallelujah praise the Lord, I am his.

Now I will tell you about my precious daddy that visited Heaven. I loved my daddy and he loved me. When I went off to college to become a teacher he was put in the hospital because they felt something was wrong. They found nothing wrong with him but that he missed me and was grieving for me. My mom was on fire for the Lord and she had been at Lee's father's Funeral and felt that presence just as I had felt it. She was serving God in a powerful church and daddy was just grieving. Daddy got saved after a few months of missing me. One day he was in the bathroom after being saved. He died and went out of the bathroom window and was standing before the pearly gates and asking, "Can I go in there?" The Angel said he would check his book for his name. All of a sudden, he heard mom calling him. "Fred, Fred", and he went back into his body. He came to on the bathroom floor and was crying and said "Why did you call me back from that beautiful place?" She hugged him and said she loved him. Mom said that for weeks and weeks he cried and wanted to go back to that beautiful place. Every day he would just sob and want to return to Heaven. Finally, one day mom came home and he was not crying and said" I am going to tell everyone about that beautiful place and get them to go to that beautiful place with me." That is what he did for the next few years. Dad got on fire for the Lord and witnessed to tons of people that crossed his path and told his story.

A lady in my Sunday School class wanted me to pray over her so I asked the Lord what I should pray for. She did not tell me what I needed to pray over. I prayed with her and let the Lord lead my mouth. The next week she catches me in the hall and screams, "I got the job that we prayed for last week." I sent praises up to my Lord for his help in this matter. I did not know what I had prayed for. God knew and allowed me to help her through Him. Sometimes we just need to trust him and he will be there to help.

A few weeks later I was in my classroom and looking up into a cabinet and the Lord spoke, "You will not be here tomorrow." I said, "But Lord no one is sick and I just don't miss school unless there is a sick child or relative." He repeated it again. I said "OK, Lord we will see." I went home everyone was fine. I went to bed and slept and the next morning I had bugs in my hair. I have long hair and they were in my hair from my first graders hugging me. I called the school to get me a sub and I had to clean up my bed, vehicle, couch and of course my head. The next day I returned to school. I parked my vehicle and my mouth dropped open in shock. I looked and every teacher's car was keyed including the Principal's car. Someone took a key and keyed the sides, the hoods, and the top. When I went into the school I asked what had happened to all the vehicles in the parking lot. They said that some middle school kids were suspended and they had nothing no better to do but to key all the cars. The teachers and Principal had to handle it through their insurance because the kids were underage. I praised the Lord for saving my vehicle from keying. He is there to protect us and keep us safe in every way he can. WOW......we serve a mighty GOD.

Teaching 1995

A day later I was in my classroom after school was over and the Librarian came down the hall and entered my room screaming, "Why did you cut off the brain of the computers on this wing?" I said I had not touched that power source. She said I had done it and I should be ashamed for telling a lie. I said I had never touched that today. I told her I had a mother putting up things on the walls in the hall and she might have disconnected it. She was using a glue gun and she might have unplugged it by mistake. I told her I was sorry.

She said, " you did it. I know you did it." Her words were so cutting because she was so angry at me. She was screaming and saying I was at fault. Finally, she plugged that brain back up and left. I cried out to my God and told him he knew I was innocent of all she claimed I had done. I got home, and I was still distraught, and I turned instantly by asking the Lord for the right scripture to heal my hurting soul. I turned in my Bible to psalms 37. I read it. Here is the scripture.

Psalms 37

Do not fret because of evil men or be envious of those who do wrong.

For like the grass they will soon wither,

Like green plants they will soon die away.

Trust in the Lord and do good; dwell in the land and enjoy safe passage.

Delight yourself in the Lord and he will give you the desires of your heart.

Commit your way to the Lord; trust in him and he will do this:

He will make your righteousness shine like the dawn,

The justice of your cause like the noonday sun.

Be still before the Lord and wait patiently for him;

Do not fret when men succeed in their ways,

When they carry out their wicked schemes,

Refrain from anger and turn from wrath; do not fret-it only leads to evil.

For evil men will be cut off, but those who hope in the Lord will inherit the land.

A little while, and the wicked will be no more; though they look for them they will not be found.......and so on....

I read this psalm and felt much better. The Lord had spoken through his word to my soul. It was healing and wonderful to know that I was innocent and unjustly accused of something I did not do. The next year this Librarian was gone and a new one took her place. This new Librarian became a close friend of mine. We would share our lives and help each other take things to our rooms from our vehicles. It was awesome to have her for my friend. The Lord's scripture helped me heal from those scathing words. She was gone and a beautiful lady took her place in the Library.

A few months later day I got out of my vehicle and I heard a hissing sound. I walked around and saw my tire going down like it had a nail in it or something else. I told the angels to keep that tire up until I finished my teaching that day and allow me to get it fixed after school. When school was over I came out and looked at the tire and it was not flat. I drove to the nearest gas station and had them put the spare on for me until I got the tire repaired. The Lord is ever present if we acknowledge him and give him the control of our lives. Thank you, Angels. God always helps us if we ask and believe.

Praying for other People and Visit by a Demon

A FEW WEEKS LATER I WAS COMING HOME FROM THE church and the Lord spoke and said as I went by a house to pray for the people in that house. It was the home of my friend Darla. So, I told him I would. I did not know why but I would start tomorrow. Then a few hundred yards down the road he spoke again and said, " Pray for these people too." I said I would and I would add them to my prayer list that I prayed over each morning on the way to school. So, I prayed every day starting with Monday, Tuesday, Wednesday, and Thursday. I prayed for those homes and people the Lord asked me to. On Thursday afternoon after I returned from school there was a doorbell ring at the back door. I answered the door and it was the guy from the second house the Lord asked me to pray for. He said, "You will not believe what happened today. Darla (from the 1st house) was riding through the neighborhood with her young son checking for anything out of order going on at any neighbor's home. She rode by her sister's house and saw a strange pickup under the carport backed up to the carport door. She turned around and went back to see what was going on at her sister's home. She got out of the car and walked towards the door on the carport. A man grabbed her by the head and drug her into the house screaming obscenities. They were slapping her and threatening to kill her with a gun raised to her

22

head. Suddenly, outside a loud crashing noise was heard. It scared the robbers and they dropped her. They thought someone was coming to catch them. (I believe the angels made that noise because of my prayers over these families). Darla was taken to the hospital with a few scrapes and scratches but no harm was done to her. They caught the men the next day. I went down to the second home and told them of my God's prompting me to pray over them since Sunday. I knew then that my prayers were for the protection of these families and to save Darla's life. I thanked Jesus, my Lord, for the prompting that He gave me.

Here is the newspaper article about this event.

LEXINGTON HOME ROBBED AND THE LORD REIGNS IN MY LIFE

TWO MEN ARRESTED

County authorities have arrested two West Columbia men in connection with a home burglary an assault that occurred Nov. 14.

Bob and Joe are incarcerated in the county Detention Center charged with one count each of first degree burglary and kidnapping. Sheriff James said the two are believed to have broken into a home on Springs road. While they were inside the residence, a concerned neighbor spotted them and went to inquire into their activity. The two men forced the neighbor, Darla, into the residence where she was struck in the head several times before the two fled the area, according to police reports. Detectives are continuing to investigate the two in connection with other crimes in the area. (11-21-96).

A few days later I was in my front yard and I came upon one of my azaleas with no leaves and scraggly looking. I viewed the rest of the yard which is full of azaleas and beautiful in April when they bloom. I realized it was dying and not healthy like all of the other azaleas. So, I prayed and put my hands on the bush and prayed, "Grow in the name of Jesus and be big and beautiful." In a few weeks, I remembered the plant and went to see if it was like it was the last time I saw it. I saw it and it was big and healthy and full of green leaves. I praised the Lord and danced joyfully. Thank you, my Lord. Today it is one of the largest azaleas in my yard. My yard is laced abundantly with many flowers but the azaleas are the biggest and most profuse of all my flowers.

A few weeks later I woke up and found a huge man standing over my bed on my side, with glaring eyes on me. I have a cathedral ceiling in my room and he looked like no man on earth; He was too big and those eyes were red and glowing. I immediately realized that he was a demon. I said, "GO IN THE NAME OF JESUS. GO BACK TO HELL WHERE YOU CAME FROM." He vanished in an instant right before my eyes. I never was afraid because I know my God will protect me from anything demonical in nature. In The name of Jesus, there is power over demons.

My Lord speaks about Lee, my dreams, and the Flu

One beautiful spring day Lee and I went fishing in our john boat and we were catching a lot of crappie up on Lake Marion. Lee decided to park the boat in a beautiful butterfly and flower garden on the water. The butterflies in the flowers were so pretty to behold. I told the Lord it was a garden on earth and on the water and I truly loved it. Lee decided to take a nap and I decided to talk to my God. I asked the Lord, "How long before he comes to know you, Lord? He needs you in his life and I want him to put his hand to the plow and never look back." The Lord spoke and said, "Lee will be in the rapture." I said," Lord, how can that happen when he is so far from you? He doesn't know you and he is so wayward and never has time for you. I hope he will know you and serve you while he is on this earth. Lord, I know nothing is impossible with you." It was many years later before Lee knew God.

Lee and I when we were young 1981

I had a dream one night of being in the rapture. I was on the clouds with a lot of children. I thought maybe this rapture will happen at school and all my little first graders will go with me. Also, I saw adults but fewer than the children. I could look at the people and communicate without opening my mouth. They could communicate with me just by looking at me. Most of all I felt the presence of God's love. The love was not like any human love found on earth or romantic love or family love. It was deeper and penetrated your soul and it satisfied me. It was sweet and deep and all loving with no hindrances. God loves us unconditionally as his child. Lee was trying to wake me up. I didn't want to leave but he was persistent. I don't think I would have remembered it if he had not awakened me. I love the joy and love I felt on that cloud. It is not of this world. It is the creator's LOVE.

A few months later I was called to school to pick up my daughter from middle school because she was very sick. I carried her to the vehicle out of the school she attended. I took her to the doctor and she had the flu. The next week I went to school and at 9:00 I was running a high fever. It came on me suddenly and I could not hold my feverish head up. I called my doctor when I arrived home and they told me to come right in. I had the flu. I felt horrible and I went home and went to bed. I had the flu and the high fever for 3 solid days. I was one miserable woman and I had no time for my God. I had never spent 3 days without my Bible, prayers, and singing to him. I got on my knees and I said, "Lord, take this fever away and let me be able to be with you. I miss you and I want you. You were in the tomb 3 days, Please, have mercy on me. Release me now that 3 days have passed and let me worship you and have my mind on you." In 30 minutes, my fever went down to 99.8 from 103. I spent time talking to my God and thanking him for his hand in my life. I thanked him for lowering my fever to a low fever and I was so happy. In 2 more days, all the fever was gone and I was back to normal. Thank you, My Jesus.

One night a few weeks later I had a dream about Lee and I. We were on a hay wagon and I was on my stomach and he was stretched out on top of me on his stomach. We were laughing and having a good time. He had his arms completely around my neck and we were so close and loving. All of a sudden, we went through a pine glen and a lightning bolt hit Lee in the ankle. Slowly, oh so slowly, his hands released my head and he rolled off the hay wagon onto the pine straw and acted as if he was dead. He was dressed in full hunting apparel. I woke up and asked myself, "What did that mean?" I called my mom and asked her to pray for Lee. I told her the dream and she prayed protection over Lee. Later in my life a few years later I realized what the dream meant. The Lord was going to come between Lee and I spiritually and it would take a few years to do it. The slow movement of Lee's arms around my head coming loose meant it would take many years to come between us. Me, strong in the Lord, and Lee running after hunting to make himself happy. Believe me God DID come between us and it was a struggle. Lee said a few years later that something had come between us and he felt it. I told him that no man would ever come between me and My God. He was real and I would never give him up.

My God speaks, Atlanta visit, and Holy Spirit's Presence

ONE FALL DAY A YEAR LATER, I WAS BUSY WITH THE children and supper and the Lord spoke and said he wanted to speak to me. I said, "OK, Lord. I will find time to meet with you. So, I went outside away from all the noise and hum of the house. I went by the back deck and said, "OK, Lord. I am ready." I waited for over 5 minutes. He was waiting until I cleared my mind for him to speak. Then he spoke, "I am coming back soon. Get busy and do my work." I said, " I will do all I can for you and I will help lead many home to be with you, when you come. You are my Savior. I will do your will." I got busy with helping others know about him. This was the first time he spoke to me about his coming.

In 2000, I visited in Atlanta the Westin Peachtree Plaza Hotel (shaped like a cylinder) to attend the End Time Handmaidens and Servants 25th World Convention. This was a life changing experience and I witnessed things I had never been a part of ever. They had a guy named Robert Shattles; when he spoke and preached, gold dust fell on his hair and shirt, and he was covered with it. He had a testimony of being a cop in Atlanta and sitting in a car with his partner on the passenger side and a man walked up to him with a gun pulled and threatened to shoot Robert. He put up his hand to shield himself from the gun. The gun went off and he shot point blank range at him.

The gunman fled away. Robert got out of the car and saw where the bullets went through the seat, but did not enter his body in anyway. He was safe because God protected him and he walked away unscathed. While Robert was preaching, a woman had a heart attack and he prayed for her and Jesus healed her. The praise and worship was with banners, shofars, twirling flags, crowns, and the ark of the covenant. This convention is headed by Gwen Shaw. She is a beautiful lady that served Jesus in the mission's field all of her life till she could not travel. Now she founded the End Time Handmaidens and Servants fellowship. They took up an offering for the Peace house in Jerusalem and got 92k and only needed 91k to pay the house off. We were in a beautiful service and my daughter saw my grandmother (the one who kept her when she was little and she had died a few years before this) on a cloud. She threw down coins and said money is worthless and Jesus is our gold. She cried when she told me. My son said he saw a big angel standing behind Mr. Shattles as he preached. Out by the pool I looked up into the sky and beside the cylinder building we were in was a white horse formed by the clouds. Benny Hinn's wife was there and she gave a testimony of being a child from 2 generations of preachers. She prayed and almost all of the people fell under the anointing. We heard the marching of soldier's feet and it was awesome. Mr. Shattles preached again and he was covered with gold dust. Then he prayed for everyone standing in a line and as he approached the people they fell to the floor and were slain in the spirit. I was slain to the floor in the spirit. I was so drunk I could not get off the floor for about 45 minutes. Jesus had me and he was holding me in his arms of love. One morning at the convention we went to a morning praise and worship and my daughter drew a picture of what she saw in praise and worship. She took it up to Gwen

Shaw and showed her. My daughter started crying and she asked her why she was crying. She said that mom, my son, and her were in the Rapture but her dad was left behind. She asked my daughter if she could call her dad Lee and talk to him. My daughter said, "NO, NO he would get mad." So, Miss Gwen had Lee prayed over by the whole world. This convention was a world convention. Many countries were represented. Then Miss Gwen looked at my daughter's picture and it was a white horse with Jesus on its back and the banner on the horse said, "The earth will shake with the Glory of the Lord." Under the horse's feet were the stones with people's faces on the stones. Miss Gwen said, "This child never knew that scripture says that they are living stones. God revealed that to her." Finally, we had to leave and go home. We packed up and left. I sensed that we had left something behind. About an hour away from Atlanta, my son had to go to the restroom and he had gold dust on his face. We found as we stopped that a bag of tapes we had purchased were missing. We called security at the hotel and told them what we had lost. I said, "Let's pray. God is trying our faith." We joined hands and prayed for restitution. The phone rang 5 minutes later and they had found the bag. So, we turned around and went back and picked up the bag. Thank you, Jesus. Never have I ever experienced anything like this before. It was life changing.

A few weeks later at school a teacher friend dropped by my room to visit and told me her sister was going to die in the hospital. I said, "Do you believe in healing?" She said, "Yes I do. I said, "Would you like for me to pray with her today after school?" She agreed and I put it on my agenda to go to that hospital and pray for her sister. After school, I went home and petitioned God on my back deck. I told him that I wanted her, the sister, to give you the credit for her healing. Don't heal her if she doesn't give you the praise. So, I went to the hospital with my Bible and met the teacher outside her room. I wanted to be sure she wanted the prayer. The teacher reassured me that she was OK with me praying. So, I went in and I laid my hands on her and prayed that she would be healed by the stripes of Jesus. The next day my teacher friend came in my room and tells me in a happy voice that her sister is getting out of the hospital TODAY. I say, "Praise the Lord for his mercy endures forever. YOU HEALED HER. THANK YOU!" I told her that the Lord Jesus healed her and not me. Give him the credit. A few years later my teacher friend is in the hospital and I go to visit her. I see sitting in the recliner beside her bed her sister with a Bible in her hand. God let me see that she did give him the credit. Praise the Lord.

Water woes and Benny Hinn Convention

One summer day I found out that my house had no water. We have a water pump in the ground. It happened in the summer when I was out of school. It went out on a Friday afternoon and Saturday I call all the water drillers I can get ahold of on a Saturday. Everyone has a waiting list of 90 days, and all the people's wells are drying up because of no rain and the ants are getting in some of the wells. I cry out to my God and told him, "I can't wait that long. I will be back in school in a month. How will we survive 90 days?" He reminds me, "Didn't I teach a well driller's son a few years back?" I said "Oh yes, I did." So, I looked up his number and gave him a call. On Monday, he calls and asks me what do I need. I say, "I need a well drilled. Mine is dried up and can you help me. There are waiting lists in my town 90 days out." He said that he had a list too, but I was at the top of that list. He would be there the next day and drill my well. By Friday, I have a beautiful water supply to my house. Thank you, Lord Jesus. Absolutely NO 90 days!

Around the time of no water, I attended a Maurice Cerullo Convention at the Sheradon Hotel. My mom meets me at the hotel and we go in to the convention. He preaches and then we stand up and he says to the left, "BE SLAIN IN THE NAME OF JESUS." The people fall as a group to the floor. Then he turns to the right where I am and he says it again and I fall with everyone else falling to the floor under the anointing. We fall together as a group to the floor like dominoes. I stay down and I am drunk in the spirit, and I can't get up. Finally, I get up and find mom but I am still very drunk and we walk to the vehicles and I can walk only sideways. I get in my vehicle and ask the Lord how to drive on the interstate drunk. He tells me to stay in the right lane and go the speed I can go. So, I go and obey Him and all of a sudden, my mouth opens and I start speaking in tongues and I can't stop myself even if I wanted to. I finally, after 10 years of being a fireball for my God I receive the gift of speaking in tongues. WOW…I have wanted these tongues and never got them until that night. God is so good all the time. Now I have another dilemma. I have to get past Lee drunk as I am and I asked my Savior about how to get past Lee. He said, "Just sit down and act normal. He is watching wrestling and he will not be as attentive to you." That was exactly what I did. I was very crooked on the sidewalk to my house. I just had to walk right in the foyer and sit down in my recliner and speak to him and then get up to get a shower. I was still a little drunk but getting better. It worked and he never knew about what happened that night……awesome time with my God.

A few weeks later I went to a Benny Hinn Convention in Charlotte. My mom and kids went with me. Before we left Lee had a fit in the parking lot not wanting us to go. I told him I had wanted to see Benny Hinn and I was going. We left and got in traffic in Charlotte close to the Convention. We were up on the top of the building and the people on the stage looked like miniature pixies. We had a beautiful worship and the songs honored my God. Then he preached, and then afterwards he called for the sick, cripple, and those needing a healing touch. He slayed the people, and they got up and were healed. On the way home, I decided I was never going to that Conference again, because I was taking up a seat that belongs to people in need. I never went back again. There are too many hurting and needing my Savior's touch. I would never keep them away by taking a seat they could occupy.

A few weeks later I went in the back yard to praise my Lord and I starting fussing, "Why do I have to do this alone?" God told me, "The grass, where are their hands?" I said, "Up." He said, "The flower's hands?" I said, "Up," He said, "the tree's hands?" I said, "Up." Then I understood that nature worships with me and I am not alone. I never ever fussed again. I today praise him outside and inside with my ipod. He loves for us to praise him and spend quality time with him. He captures our voices and it is a sweet aroma for him in Heaven. He also captures our prayers and they are a sweet aroma for him. So, anything you do for him he knows, captures, and treasures it. Psalms 56:8 says Our tears are kept in a bottle and recorded.

We teachers have aides in our classrooms because our numbers are greater than 18. So that year I had a Godly aide with me in my classroom.

A few weeks later my aide in my classroom was absent and I felt in my spirit that I needed to pray for her. She laid very heavy on my heart. When I had a break from the children I prayed protection over her and that the Lord knew that what I was praying for would protect her. The next day she came back to school and we talked about it and she said she came very close to taking her life because of the extreme pain from a migraine headache. The Lord prompted me to pray for this woman of God that faced a decision that I knew nothing about but sensed that I needed to pray. He leads us to pray even if we don't know what we are praying for.

MY MOTHER HONORS ME AND MY FAITH INCREASES

I WILL TELL YOU NOW ABOUT A TIME I WAS HONORED BY my mom for being the only Christian in our home. It was Mother's Day and I went down to the town my mom lives in to attend church with her to honor her on this special day. I still do this till this day because I want to honor her in a special way on Mother's Day. We went to church and had a lunch together and then we gave our Mother her gift. This happened at my sister's home. Mom and my sister live next door to each other. My brother was there also honoring mom. My mom read in Proverbs 31:1-31. It is about the wife of noble character. She told me I was that woman in that scripture. She was telling me that she honored my responsibility of taking my children to church and bringing them up in the admonition of the Lord. I was the only parent serving God at that moment. I was truly touched by this gesture and knew that I truly was a mother like that wife. Wow I truly was cherished.

My sister, my Brother, and me

A few weeks later, down in Charleston, Lee and I went fishing off the coast out to reefs that held fish because of the structure in the water. We left one reef and went to another reef and as we were traveling I looked up and saw a beautiful angel with flowing hair, sandaled feet, a long robe with a scarlet sash, about 10 feet up in the air over the water. I closed my eyes and shook my head as if I could not believe what I had seen. When I opened my eyes, she was gone. I asked Lee if he had seen anything and he said, "Not a thing." I will never forget her beautiful hair golden and flowing in the air. As a result of this encounter I started collecting angel figures and I put them in a curio that is in my home today. All the angels I collected are very much like what I saw, and she had wings just like my figurines do. I can feel at all times I am not alone. My angel is always there and helping me when I need help. I sometimes can't get out of the road and merge with traffic so I call on the Lord to help me and the traffic lessens and I can merge.

A few weeks later I was in my back yard and I had a vision of a person in a bed. It was a female because of the long hair. I asked the Lord if it was me. He said, "No." I asked if it was my daughter. He again said, "No." I was happy to know it wasn't in my immediate family. So, I let it pass and didn't know who it was. That vision took place in the spring. In the fall, my sister got sick and she had to have a throat operation. I knew then who it was. She went in the hospital and had her throat operated on. I prayed everything would go great for her, and it did except she felt a coldness from the man she was with at that time. She found out that he did not care for her like he should. It was a wakeup call for her.

The children and I decided one day at school to honor the veterans in our town. We made cards and I let each child make up a card to give to a veteran that we picked out to honor. We sent the cards in a manila folder in the mail to our veteran. He was so delighted by our gesture that he sent us a lovely card, and thanked us for our honoring him and giving him a smile for our efforts and thoughtfulness. We were so honored by his response. Here is the card in reply to our cards from this veteran.

> I would like to thank Mrs. Springer's First grade class for all the beautiful cards. Each card had such a heart-felt message that put a smile on my face. I look forward to Veteran's Day every year because I know I served my Country with honor and pride. I'm sorry this card is just getting to you all but I

am grateful that you all took time out of your day to honor me. Again, Thank You.

Mr. Washington

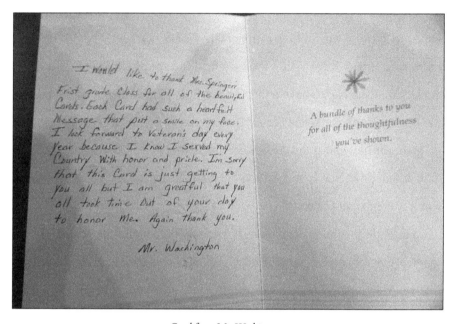

Card from Mr. Washington

Every March Lee and I would go to the tax man and get our taxes done. Lee had a business and I had school income so we went together. One particular time after we left the office of the tax man he jumped on me and accused me of throwing my money away in that church. I was giving 10% to my church because that is God's requirement, and I was not going to quit. He went on and on in the car until I decided I was turning to my God. A few days later I asked my God what I needed to do. I was obeying him and Lee was not happy that I was tithing. So, he said to me loud and clear, "Just

LOVE him". That was not what I wanted to hear. I obeyed my God and the next year no fussing came up about my tithing. He loves us and helps us in the right way. I always obey him.

After this episode, I needed help in loving Lee. So, I asked God for help. He told me to find that Fascinating Womanhood book and put it to practice in my life. I remembered the book and I looked everywhere for it. It was nowhere to be found. Then I remembered that I had let a teacher borrow it and her house had burned down. So, I started looking for it in Christian bookstores and could not find it. One day I was shopping for some books at the Christian bookstore to read and got ready to check out, and put my books on the counter to check out and there in front of me was the book. The Lord placed it right in front of me and I bought it and applied it to my life and no fussing from Lee again. The name of the book that the Lord wanted me to use was Fascinating Womanhood by Helen Andelin. You can purchase it still today. It teaches how to treat and think about a man and how to value him, admire him, and make him feel special. It truly works.

A few months later on a glorious beautiful day in the spring, I was out in my front yard (several acre front yard) with pretty flowers like a garden hiding from Lee so I could praise my Lord. I was enjoying my praising my God, and then a bee bit me and it hurt. I told the Lord that was not fair. I had to hide and be able to praise him on my cassette player. I asked him to take the sting away and let me continue with my praise to him. He took the sting away and I enjoyed the rest of my day with my God. He is so Goooooooood.

After school a few days later, we met as a first grade to discuss the next year. One of the teachers decided to tell me that I was going to have a "witch" as an aide in my class with me next year. She would be mean and ugly with

41

the children. My aide was retiring and that is why I would have a new one next year. Well, I decided to answer her. I said, "I serve a higher power (with my finger pointing up to Heaven), Jesus Christ, and that will never happen. I do not claim that." The next year I had a sweet loving Christian lady with me and they saw for themselves that it did not happen. Praise the Lord. I do not accept curses pronounced on me. I refute any bad words pronounced over me. I do this every day of my life. It is the mantra of my life to not accept those bad words. I serve a higher power that protects me from those words. Praise the Lord Jesus!

Teaching my little angels

Lumina Van Woes

FOR TWO YEARS I WISHED FOR A BLUE LUMINA VAN. IT
was the answer to kids, plenty of room, and I could take half of my class with
me on field trips. I finally got my wish two years later on May 13, 1994. It was
brand new, blue, and plush. I loved every inch of my van. On September 13, it
broke down on me and I had to be towed to the nearest Chevrolet dealership.
The bottom line was it had a bad computer. They replaced the computer and
I thought everything was great. One year later it broke down and had to be
towed to the same dealership. Again, a computer was the problem. I told them
to find out what was killing the computer. They did everything to find out and
came up emptyhanded. Being a Christian, I then prayed to my Lord about
keeping the van. He told me strike 3 and the van is gone. I said, "Ok, Lord,
I will." Six months later my van broke again and had to be towed. I knew
in my heart that this was strike 3, and the van is gone. I cried and petitioned
the Lord, and spent many hours saying this is the last time. This time they
will fix it for good. I made myself believe that is was fixed finally. I forgot
the Lord's strike 3 answer and pushed it out of my mind. Three months later,
on the way to church all alone on the interstate my van broke down again. I
came to a stop on the interstate on the median. I looked up to Heaven and
said, "I hear you, Lord, loud and clear. You got my attention this time. I will
get rid of it. This van is keeping me away from YOU. I promise you this day

it will go. Nothing comes between you and me. I mean it with all my heart and soul. I spent the next 6 months looking for something to replace my van. Lee suggested a Tahoe. I started looking and found a beautiful one close to my home in my neighborhood. We bought it and put the van up for sale. The van was for sale August, September, and October. Not one call. Lee had given me 6k towards my Tahoe till my van sold. I was getting desperate. He had been generous in helping me get out of the van. I knew I needed to sell the van as soon as I could. Finally, in church in early November the church wanted to retire the debt on a building. I pledged 500$ to the building fund and to my Lord that Sunday. I arrived home from church and the phone was ringing. A lady wanted to buy my van. She had to get a ride out to my house. At 7pm she arrived and looked at the van and said, "Take the sale signs down. This van is sold." I said, "Don't you want to hear it run?" she said, "No, I want this van. It is beautiful." She came into the house and paid 10K cash on a Sunday night. No banks were open. She had 10k in cash and Lee mentioned that it had to be from the Lord. I paid the church 500$ the next Sunday and gave Lee his 6K. I was so surprised that the Lord delivered me from a van that was a nightmare in just 3 hours. The Tahoe was also a gift from my Lord. It was bought by those folks, the sellers, on my birthday off the showroom floor of Love Chevrolet and I paid 2 years later half of what they paid. I had a warranty on the truck and it was a very reliable and dependable vehicle. God is soooo good. Thank you, Lord. I learned a lesson by this event that I was never to buy another vehicle without asking my Lord to help me. And to this day I ask and I receive beautiful vehicles that are dependable. He is waiting and willing to help.

Sylvester, Our Cat

THIS IS AN ARTICLE WRITTEN BY MY DAUGHTER.....
about our cat, Slyvester

It was a rather cool, blustery day that morning. The sun hadn't pulled back the covers just yet. It was about 7:40 in the morning. We had already taken my brother to school, and we were sitting in our driveway. Just an average day waiting in my Dad's Suburban to board the rickety old school bus to take me to school. Or so I thought. Slightly shivering, I looked up at my dad as he looked stealthily on towards the direction of the oncoming bus, that you can hear a mile away. Then something very fast caught my eye there in the street ..a black shimmer, a sort of blur. And all I could see as I looked up was that big red hulk of a vehicle speeding onwards, barreling straight for that black blur. A black blur that could not move held back by time that seemed to stop at that very moment…a screech and then my thoughts were dazed. What had just happened? It all seemed a mystery, until I looked up. There, by the side of the road, appearing lifeless, a void of black fur, my cat. There was nothing I could do, and a flood of hopelessness swept over me. I stopped spellbound, caught up by the emotion of the moment, and starting heaving big tears. It was just a cat, but I was a cat lover. And this was my favorite. There, laying lifeless, and then just a little movement in the right back leg and then, a jolt across the road and he was gone. Still, my bus driver had no idea why I was crying the way I had been when she pulled up. In a tizzy she asked my father, "What is the matter?" I just kept on crying and praying, praying to see those staring, beautiful, golden eyes again. My dad let the bus creep on by, tens of eyes staring down at me in wonder. Some of those eyes would become a comfort to me as I learned and grew at a new school I would love and miss. I was new at this school and so was everyone else, so unsure of what had just currently happened. My dad finally shook me from his shoulder, only to see my face, stained red by the steady stream of tears that just could not stop. If all creatures had a right to live, I kept thinking, this one surely did. To make me more secure that my cat would be alright, and to get my thoughts distracted from the events just starting my day, he took me to McDonald's. a restaurant I have loved ever since a kid. The golden arches were like a grandma's arms that morning ..all loving and inviting , as a stream of golden sunshine's light filtered through the windows warming my shoulders. As I gathered my thoughts we grabbed an ice cold OJ, steaming hash browns, and two scrumptious breakfast burritos. To sit in that warm McDonald's to eat. This did give me a better insight on my day. One of those hash browns I stashed in my book sack for safekeeping. When we left that McDonald's that blustery day, under the full guidance of the blazing sun, I had peace, a reassurance that my world would not fall apart. That indeed my world would be mended back together. Those golden arches still held me close as I hopped into the Suburban. When we arrived at school, I felt so much better. My friends questioned what had made me cry so much, and sheepishly I told them that it had been my cat. Then all the sad, long-forgotten pet stories came rolling in and hugs all to help me feel better. In fact, I had never felt better. My friends never left me out and sometimes they would call me the "Leader of the Pack." In first block, I had set my mind up that I would go on a safari hunt for that cat. I was getting antsy when that dismissal bell ran at 3:20. Rushing down the corridors with the other hustle and bustle of screaming teens I boarded the bus, waiting and hoping that mom would be home. When I had to get off, I had to get off on the side of the road that Sylvester had crossed, the side he was on. Looking for a second, I thought of those gorgeous, golden eyes that looked at me so sweetly the day before. Instead I saw a familiar silver Cadillac., Ms. Peggy's vehicle, parked in the yard. She was our babysitter. Concerned, and a devoted animal lover herself, she and my brother, joined in the on the hunt across the street. I knew the general direction in which the black blur had catapulted itself; so we begin. We carried only a box and net by hand, and hope and my prayer in our back pockets. We went down only a small portion of the road, looking and calling for him. Then we had to turn back because we knew that my mom would be back from work at school very soon. We headed across the road to see the blue-green Tahoe already parked in the yard. The first thing I said was not, "Hello" but "I need your help." Ms. Peggy told us before she left to be careful. Now, we carried a bigger box across the street. The only thing scaring me was what we would find. A whole day had almost gone by and I was unaware of his physical condition. As soon as we hit pay dirt across the street, my brother and I started yelling as hard as we could for our cat "Sylvester!" "Here kitty, kitty!" Kitty, kitty, kitty!" Mom was the one to hear it first….A weak "Meowwwww." Then, the sound drifted into my ears too. All became still as a small bird twitted softly to the dropping sun. Then again, a soft but steady "Meowww." We all heard it this time. I spun around in all directions confused and maddened. "Where is he?" I asked. Mom pointed. And there, lying in a bush and straw, propped up against a tree was Sylvester, black fur glistening in the afternoon sun. He was bleeding in his eye pretty bad. He was limp as I lifted him into the box, but I could feel a power in those legs, and he wasn't yelping in pain. He was still in "shock" from what had happened to him, and he wasn't quite himself. We carried him across the street. I kept praising God that he was still alive and that we had found him. He didn't like car rides. My brother and I had to hold the cat down from severing the box from top to bottom with his giant claws. No, I was certain he would be alright from the "yowwww's" he made and the abrupt kicks produced on the trip to the vet. After only a few minutes the vet came up with a crystal- clear diagnosis. He would need stitches in the corner of his eye, and some medication for his soreness. No broken bones and no internal bleeding. I was amazed beyond belief. So was my dad. You had to be there to see it and not to believe the doctor was right, but he was! The red Dodge truck's tires had just somehow nicked him in the eye. He had out run the two huge front tires of a Dodge truck! After that, I was no longer scared for his sake, but I was rejoicing! The day he came home was the day I had first realized just how lucky he had been. He doesn't have nine lives, but friends in high places. Like the angels that helped him across the road. He truly is a miracle cat. I think because he is built so strong and has such big bones, the way God had specially designed him with perfect skill, was the reason he lived. The fact that an angel or maybe even ten were right there at that precise second, the very boost he needed to get out of harm's way was a definite factor in his victory over death! No more does my cat ever go near that road. No more trips across the road looking for his cat friends to hang out with. There is no other way to describe what I had witnessed other than a true act of God, saving my cat from certain danger. Now, Sylvester is as happy as lazy as any other cats in the neighborhood. He is the kind of cat you love and adore and who always sticks with you, just like one of your best pals. To keep him strong I feed him a half bowl of cat food and he just purrs with delight as I stroke his back. And I, I thank God and I am proud for the chance to own a miracle cat with a set of wings!

I (the author) got this cat from a lady that said he would not stay home. He was only a year old. He was a Maine Coon cat. I needed a cat to stand up to a big- headed cat that was terrorizing my kittens and cats. We had 3 cats to die from that cat attacking them. So, I told the Lord I needed a big cat that could stand up to that mean cat. When we got Sylvester, he would confront any cat that came into our yard. If they got close he would roll himself and them into a ball, and roll across the yard like a bowling ball. One day I stepped out on the front porch and the porch came alive with the fur all over the porch. Sylvester had defurred a cat that came too close. He loved to stand out in the rain and get wet. We realized his fur was rain repellant. One time it snowed and he stayed out in the snow and he had large icicles hanging from his fur. He was the first to check out the pool when it was being put in. He loved water. He also raided the bird nests and they always swooped at him, and one day I found him in the back yard up in the tree raiding a bird's nest. Five or six birds were swooping down on him and trying to peck him. He was a gift from God. That day he got ran over when we were over across the street I prayed, "Lord, we don't find him if he is dead. If he is alive let us find him. Please, Lord, for the children's sake." As you know, we found him and he was not hurt very bad at all. God is so good when we ask him to help us. That mean cat never came into our yard again. Sylvester rules the Springer Yard!

Sylvester, our cat

The Doctor's Woes and my Life with the Holy Spirit

I WOULD LOVE TO SHARE A TIME MY SON WAS SICK AND I had to take him to the doctor in the fall. He was about 8 years old. They took us back at the doctor's office and I talked to the people about why they were there. One lady said her daughter (a baby) had rashes on her hands and knees. One lady said her son had a bad knee that he had fell on. My son had a cold that he could not get rid of. I was afraid it would turn into bronchitis. It did when he was younger. Then they sent all of us back to the lab. We all had the same doctor. They put a tongue depressor in the baby's throat and she just wailed and cried at the top of her lungs. I felt so sorry for that child. That baby had rashes from crawling on the carpet. They were checking for mono. I knew that was not right. Then they took blood from my son and he fainted. Never have they done this test on my son for a cold. The other mother had a mono test done on her son and a blood test on him too. I felt that these children were being put through tests that they did not need. Remember the lady with the son that had a scraped knee. I felt as if these were tests this doctor had drummed up to take more money from the insurance company. When it was time to go the doctor told me he was not giving my son anything to help him. So, on the way home I cried out to my God and I said "Prick his heart. Prick him and let him know what he is doing is wrong on the backs of little children. They are being put though unnecessary tests for him and his pocket." I cried and I cried for those precious children he was putting through those tests. When I arrived home the phone rang. I picked up and it was that doctor. I said "You better be careful because God doesn't like you drumming up charges on the backs of little children. You are using God's little ones to pay for that condo at the beach. Something terrible is going to happen to you if you don't stop drumming up charges by putting on the kids tests that make them faint and scream. My heart goes out to those kids. I would not like to be you. Sir, I will pray that you turn from this practice and do the right thing." ....After that I felt that I had stood up for the children that were being abused for money. In the spring, I told you I had the flu. When I went back in the spring I was sitting in the drug part of the doctor's office waiting on my prescription. All of a sudden, the double doors opened in front of me and I saw the most powerful lawyer in our town standing by a man in a wheelchair and they were calling for that doctor that I had told about something terrible happening to him. I said, "Lord you told me to tell him and I did." The Lord allowed me to see that restitution was in progress. I said to the Lord that you pay for those sins and I prayed that the Lord would help him change and become a fantastic doctor. I asked the Lord to help him and bring him into his kingdom. A year ago, I was reading in the paper about this doctor and how he was loved and honored by the people. My heart lit up and I was joyful that he had made the changes that he needed to do. I thanked the Lord for helping me love him.

I once told the Lord that I definitely regretted about not knowing him all of my life. If I could change something it would be to have known him from a child up into adulthood. He told me I would not understand the "lost" if I had never been that way before. I can help them more and know why they will not make that decision to know him. I understand what he was telling me and have found that it is true.

I sometimes had a meeting on Wednesday and would have to stay later for over two hours and I could not pick the children up from after school. All the other days I picked them up at the homework center at their school. My children did not go to the school I taught in. I had a babysitter on Wednesday that would meet my children at the bus and bring them to the house and keep them until I got home. It was Christmas and I wanted to get the babysitter a gift from our family. I went to a store and found some pretty towels for the bathroom. I asked the Lord which color to choose for her. I gave them to her and she commented that I had never been to her house and how did I know the color scheme of her bathroom. They matched better than any towels she had. I told her, "The Lord told me." She was amazed at the Lord helping me choose the right color.

My daughter was interested in getting the Baptism of the Holy Spirit. While I was in the restroom she had the Sunday school class pray for her to get the Baptism. When I arrived, she was speaking in another language and was prophesizing about a sheep that had eyes that were worlds spinning in its head. She said the sheep ran out into the world to share the gospel to the world. My daughter saw a woman healed the week before and she got hungry for God. She received everything the Lord gives to us in one swoop. I had to wait 10 years before I got my speaking in another language after the Morris Cerillo conference. I had the Baptism of the Holy Spirit when the Lord breathed down my back in that 2nd church. My daughter got everything. Wow …..thank you, Lord. The next page is a poem my daughter wrote shortly after this incident. The poem is about the pond that my mom owns and she as a child visited there a lot. She wrote this and it was so good so I wanted to let you read the poem that she wrote.

THE POND

(This is a poem my daughter wrote about my mom's pond.)

A place where people and animals coexist

Where you can forget your problems

At least while you are here.

I never want to forget this place

Though my eyes will dim with blindness

When I age and my hair turns white as snow.

But I trust in one thing ..I will not forget it

For it is forever in me …it is in my heart.

The trees still embrace me when I turn to leave

And the laughter of afternoon talks fade.

It is a place of memories made and forgotten.

It is green with life as a bird's wild exotic songs

Linger on my ears like the sensation of a sweet unforbidden kiss.

A breath of the air brings peace to a shaking heart and unsteady soul.

The beauty of God's mastery is shown in the life here.

Sadness and anger can't live in a place of so much life and vibrancy.

The wind is renewal of the heart.

The sun is a sweet warm heat encircling your shoulders.

The pond's water washes away impurity with its baptizing powers

Even the trees lift their arms to the sky in reverence of all God has created here.

No, I never want to lose this place though time ticks on and memories fade.

I have to face the facts of growing up but the place grows inside me,

Its trees and water and air and life live inside me.

I know I will always close my eyes and remember

These beautiful morning walks lest God take away what I love that is so deep within me.

Life flows within the chasms of the pond's water; It delves up from the ground And is instilled in you and me.

The golden sun on green countryside will be forever in my heart and the fact that God provides

And takes care of all he loves-even the flower.

Authored by Casey Springer

LOVING MY LORD

A FEW WEEKS LATER AND ON A SUNDAY THE PASTOR preached about idols that control your life. He taught about the ones that the Israelites faced in their lives and how they bowed down to stone and things made by human hands. Then he told us about the idols that we have are no different than they were back then. Whatever occupies your life and that you spend a lot of time with is an idol. I felt as if I had no idols in my life. I was smug in my feelings about this issue. He stepped behind the scenes and rolled a TV out into the room. My mouth fell open and I realized what he was teaching. I place that TV in my face a lot. I was struck by his display and realized you can make a TV your idol. Today it would be the internet and cell phones for most people. Whatever takes up your time and space in this world is an idol. So, I found that TV shouldn't be my idol. I read his word, prayed to him, praised him, and read books that helped me with my faith. TV is not the primary item that gets my attention today.

Our church was still having those theatrical plays and they gave us lots of tickets to give out for people to attend. So, I got about 25 and the kids and I put them on the windshields of the cars and trucks that we came across on our way back from Church. One day I was at the oil place getting my vehicle's oil changed. I had some of those tickets from the Church and I struck up a conversation with a group of ladies sitting in the waiting room. After talking for about 15 minutes I asked them if they wanted a ticket to attend the program at my Church and they said, "Of course." I gave them the tickets and was happy for them. This is the show that drew me to this Church to get on fire for God. After a while another 2 people came in to sit and wait and I struck up a conversation with them. We talked and I offered the tickets to them. They snapped back at me and said that they did not believe and no they did not want the tickets. I was crushed to say the least. On the way back home, I cried and wept because they did not want my tickets. God spoke and said, "I gave them free choice. Please don't ever cry again. You did what I wanted and offered and that is all I expect. Just offer and that is all you do." I knew then that free choice is important to every person and I can't get upset because they choose to not believe. God taught me a lesson I have never forgotten. People have free choice. I am obeying when I offer anything that God prompts me to do.

A few months later I went on a trip to another town to check out new teaching techniques with a group of teachers from my school. We went in a van and were having a good time going to this town. On the way, the driver, a teacher, cracked a joke about my God and everybody laughed except me. I said to myself "Father, forgive them for they know not what they say." We arrived at the school and watched the teachers using this new method and liked it very much. It became the method that we started using the very next year and I saw a big difference in the learning of my children. They excelled under this new method and I had no retentions after we implemented this idea. This new idea was instead of having 3 reading groups and branding children as smart or lower we started whole group instruction. This instruction made children feel very comfortable and no branding on levels. We used 4 blocks of instruction. The 1ˢᵗ block was snapping, clapping and stomping the words for that week and also writing the words. They learned to spell the word and use it in a sentence. Then we put the words on the word wall under the letter they started with. Then the 2ⁿᵈ block consisted of reading as a group the text of the story for the week. Those words we used in the 1ˢᵗ block were the words we practiced snapping and so on were inside the story that week. The 3ʳᵈ block consisted of a standard that we were to work on all week. It could be characters, predicting outcomes, main idea, or any other reading comprehension skill that we were instructed by standards to cover. The 4ᵗʰ block was teaching children how to write and use an outline to lay out the idea for the writing into a format that would help them pre-think the story they were to tell or the idea of a writing that explained a concept or main idea. A few weeks later I entered the run off room and overheard the conversation that was going on as I came in to run off papers for my class. They were talking about the teacher that was driving that day and they said her daughter was found drinking on a class trip with the school. I had taught this child in 1ˢᵗ grade years before. She was not going to be able to walk with her class on Graduation day. I prayed, "Lord, have mercy, please." She was a living doll when I taught her. I later found out she got to walk and she was forgiven for making one mistake. Thank you, my Jesus.

A few weeks later I was sitting in the swing on my front porch, falling leaves falling at my feet from the persimmon tree petitioning, my Lord, about Lee and crying and crying. I was asking, "How much longer will he take to become a believer?" The Lord spoke, "When you see these leaves fall off this tree next time you will find a change in Lee." I said, "Wow, Lord I am happy to hear that. I feel that next Fall he will be serving you. Thank you and I am glad to hear that." In the Spring, the persimmon tree put out leaves, and they all turned black and fell off the tree. This had never happened to this tree ever. A man from Lee's past called and Lee met him. When he returned he had some evil tapes that man had given him to listen to. I told him that they were very evil, and he better get rid of them or something bad was going to happen to him. Lee got to coughing and could not seem to sleep and it was bad for Lee. He never told me what had happened to him with this man until close to his death. He told me that man had gave him ACID to drink, and he thought it was drugs like he usually gave Lee. The Lord was right. There was a big change in Lee and it was that his health was changing. I never knew that this occurred until he was making the last trip to the hospital. The Lord is good. He prepares us for the future.

A few weeks later on a rainy day at school I was taking my kids to the bus lot to meet their bus to go home. I had an umbrella with me and I did not have bus duty. If you had bus duty you had to be on the bus lot until all bus drivers were on their buses and all kids loaded. I saw a new little teacher on duty standing in the rain with no umbrella; So, I told her to take mine and I would duck into the hall and miss the rain. She was so thankful and I went back to my classroom and was preparing for the next day and the little teacher came and told me that I had done a kind act, and thanks for the help. I told her anytime she needs me just call on me. I will help you in any way I can. I made a friend that day.

A few weeks later one morning I was driving to school praying for others like I do every day. I rounded the corner and a large logging truck loaded with trees was in my lane. I had to drive off the pavement to keep from hitting him. I thanked my God for sparing me. On the way back home, I parked my vehicle by the road and walked up to the curb I met the truck in, and realized that one inch further on the grass I would have encountered no level area but a valley that would have turned my truck over. I may not have lived. I would have rolled and rolled down that valley. I realize that life can be over in a heartbeat. God was not through with me yet.

I had another fire dream and it happened next door to my classroom. I dreamed I was walking up the hallway in my school past a kindergarten classroom. I walked into my room and saw a fire roaring through the electric plate that was between the 2 classes into the kindergarten classroom. The plate had melted and I could see the fire next door in that kindergarten classroom. It was making a high- pitched noise and just burning profusely. I woke up and realized that I needed to pray for that teacher and her aide. I prayed that they would be ok. The next day I caught that teacher and asked her if anyone in her family was sick. She said, "No, but her aide was on death's bed." I told her about my dream and she was in awe. I really prayed for the aide to recover but I heard later she had died. All in his will.

My Lord's Intervention in Lee's Life

In 2003, I had a very vexing dream and it really concerned me. I was at the beach and in bed. At 4am I was awakened in this dream by a clap of thunder. The dream was set at a school parking lot. Lee and my son were in his Suburban on one side of a chain linked fence. I was on the other side in my Tahoe. All of a sudden, I heard a shot ring out and I saw my son bail out of the Suburban and he was covered in blood. I jumped out of my Tahoe and ran to him and screamed, "My baby my baby". The fence kept us apart. Lee had committed suicide by laying a gun up to his head and firing and the blood splattered all over my son. I sat straight up in the bed and asked the Lord "What did that mean?" I was really concerned about Lee. I kept that dream in my heart and never told him about it. I made sure I never left him for any extended time. I called off a beach vacation in October. I knew the Lord was warning me of something EXTREME was getting ready to happen. It did clarify the future.

A few months later Lee and I took our boat to the Charleston Harbor Marina. We spent the night in the boat. We had a very happy time together. Lee saw a boat he wanted to go fishing with, and talked to the owner of the boat and visited his boat. We took our boat off shore and I got very scared. It was very rough and he turned back. We rode by the Charleston Battery, past

Charleston Row, and by California Dreaming. It was one of the last times that we spent together and enjoyed ourselves. Next the dream was getting ready to take place.

This event took place in May, 2003 a year I will never forget. When we arrived back home Lee washed the boat to get the salt off the boat from our trip to Charleston. He and the kids had a water fight by the boat. They were so happy. Lee came to the front porch and was talking to me about our daughter's first date. A few days later Lee and I were on the front porch and a parent called me and I talked to the parent. After I hung up Lee criticized the way I spoke to the parent (first time ever). He brought tears to my eyes and hurt me with his words. He left and went upstairs and threw a few things around up there. He stormed around mad for a while. He left at 2am to meet that guy he met in Charleston to go offshore fishing with him. He was still upset with me. He had been drinking alcohol and his bad side was showing.

The next morning, I went to school not worrying or praying for Lee. I told the Lord that I was innocent and I did not like the way he was drinking and hurting me. Everything at school went great. I returned home and talked with my kids about Lee's anger. My daughter felt that he was mad at her for that first date. I reassured her that he was not angry about that but with me. She had worn the first ring Lee had given me when we first met to school. We bonded. We all went to bed around 10pm. Lee returned home about 30 minutes later. I didn't know he was home. I slept the whole night until 5am. I awoke and started praying. I went up front and found Lee on the couch. He was sweating, feverish, and had filled a bucket 1/3 full of blood he had coughed up down by the shop. It did not register to my mind exactly what he was telling me. I put him to bed and told him to go to the doctor. I told him to call me if he needed me at school. School is 20 minutes away. I told the Office at school that Lee was sick and if he called let me know.

He had spent the whole day offshore with another boat owner. They caught 7 tuna, wahoo, dolphin, and marlin. Some of those fish Lee had never caught before on his boat. Lee took 4 aspirin to feel better. He said he felt sick at 5am at the landing in Charleston. When I arrived home, Lee was still in the bed. He had not gone to the doctor because he was too dizzy. I called the doctor and they told me to call 911 because he had lost so much blood. He told me to look in the bucket by the bed and there was another one down by the shop. Both buckets were ½ to 1/3 full of blood he had vomited up. He told me he had blood in his stool. The para medics arrived. They took him to the hospital. I sat up front in the ambulance with the driver while they worked on Lee. My kids drove their car to the hospital. He had very low blood pressure.

We got to the hospital and they told me to sit in the ER waiting room. I cried because he was losing blood and I felt he was dying and did not know my God. Prayer was hard to come by because I was in shock. They called me back and his vitals were awful. They asked me if he wanted the Clergy. I said, "If it was me, yes, but you need to ask him." They asked and he said, "YES." My mom and sister arrived and stayed with me. Lee was so critical. They worked on him nonstop. Lee was yellow in color. I went home to retrieve my Tahoe. I went back and he was moved right outside ICU. They gave him a blood transfusion. I was not leaving him until I felt he was better. I did not sleep at all.

The next morning mom arrived and they took him to get the light down him to determine what was causing the bleeding. The doctor came out and with big eyes and a pointed finger and wild hair said to me and mom, "If he takes another drink it will kill him. I have never seen veins as large as his are. I am putting rubber bands around the veins to keep them from bleeding into his stomach. I think it is cirrhosis of the liver." We were shocked at the doctor's words. Lee had told me at home that the blood he coughed up looked like a guy he knew that had died from cirrhosis of the liver. My sister told me that she had a dream where a spigot was pouring out blood the night before this incident. I cried and I felt I might be left behind. I felt Lee might die.

I looked for insurance papers and talked with mom about what to do if he died. It was very hard to face. We didn't tell the kids. Lee asked me, Is it a tumor, cancer, cirrhosis?" I said, "I wasn't going to lie….it could be cirrhosis." He told me to go home to be with the children. When I got home my son was putting up the fish Lee had in a cooler. When I went to my room it smelled like death. I sprayed air freshener into the air in my room. I had a hard time sleeping. The next day the doctor took the light down Lee and placed the rubber bands on his extremely large veins. The doctor told me that in 3 weeks he would have to have it done again. He said, "No alcohol." Later that day I shared some times the Lord had worked in my life. I shared a few of the stories that I wrote in this book. I returned home and felt better in my bed. I starting coughing about 4:30 and couldn't sleep. I knelt beside our bed and petitioned My Savior to save Lee's life. God said, "Stand up. He will live." I was so happy and I couldn't wait to tell Lee about what God had told me. I told Lee that he would live. Lee said, "All this living is foolishness. I will never take another alcoholic drink ever. I will sell the boat and live differently." He told the kids to smash all the alcohol bottles. My daughter agonized over her father. She wanted to bust up his liquor bottles and give him a chance to live. I told her that Lee had to give permission and she waited till he said she could do it.

On the 2nd Sunday afternoon in the hospital Lee had a total of 25 visitors and they had him laughing and enjoying their company. Lee's brother came with his son to share Jesus with him. It was very moving and anointed. Lee sent me home at 8pm. He wanted me to let him be alone. I had a peaceful night's sleep. The doctor told us Lee could go home Tuesday. Mom and I had lunch at the hospital and said that Lee would be saved by himself. We returned from lunch and the pastor from his brother's church came in and spoke with Lee. Lee told him that Sunday night Joel Osteen was on TV, and he gave his life to God. I was so happy I wanted to dance. Lee had finally made the decision to have God in his life. How long have I agonized, prayed and interceded for his life. My prayers were finally answered. I asked Lee to walk me to the elevators. He did and we kissed good-bye. I told him he had made me the happiest woman on earth. On Tuesday Lee was allowed to go home. He gave all his flowers to the nurses and the patients. I was so happy he was going home to serve my Jesus. When we arrived home, I shared Jesus with him and prayed with him.

After getting home Lee was swelling in his stomach. I prayed for his swelling and coughing. Lee and I watched Christian TV and that was a first. I wanted to share the Rapture with Lee. I found Lee kneeling and praying for the first time in the living room. A few days later we talked about the Lord for 3 hours. I felt a tenderness in Lee that I had never seen before. Mom and my sister visited and shared the Lord with Lee. He apologized to my sister and my mom. He is so different and has made an about face and is truly serving my God. I finally got to share in the Bible about the Rapture. He was so attentive and truly desired to know.

The dream I had was so true. God was showing me that Lee was angry at me and the fence represented that and the Blood was all that we encountered when he had his brush with death. My son was directly affected by the close call showing the blood on him. God will always be there no matter what we face. He had my hand when I traversed through that valley, and came out on the other side smiling. I could not have faced this milestone in my life without his hand in mine.

Lee stopped drinking. He dropped all his party buddies. He started going to church with me but did not want to go to the church I had attended because he felt like he had been prayed over a lot there. That was no lie. I had him prayed over thousands of times. Lee started reading the Bible and my family could easily talk about the Lord when they visited. He helped my sister with her house to get rid of mice coming in her home. He sealed up holes where they were gaining access to her home. He fixed other people's decks and never told me about it. I found out after his death. He had made the biggest changes and my last 4 years were beautiful with him. I was free to share with him how the Lord helps me and how he is there for me. I had to go to a baby church because the Lord told me I needed Lee to drink milk and then he would grow in his faith. So, we went to a church where he was fed milk. I needed deeper preaching so my mom copied for me some videos of Benny Hinn. I had a TV video package in my kitchen and while I was cooking supper I would listen to him. That helped me grow in my walk with the Lord. I felt I was getting fed and deepening my walk with the Lord.

Lee continued with the bandings. We every 6 weeks had to go to the out-patient of the hospital and have his veins rubbered banded. After about a year he stopped the bandings and Lee never had any trouble with that again. He also got a condition called ascites. He had fluid to fill up his stomach cavity and we would have to go and get it syphoned off by sticking a needle in and draining his stomach. He had this condition for the last 3 years of his life. Lee's faith grew and he became a peaceful man and a joy to be with. I truly loved my husband and his newfound faith. It truly made me a happy woman and I remained that way the rest of my time with him. We went one night to hear a gospel group at his brother's church and he enjoyed that very much.

Lee told me he had asked the Lord about if he would live or not. Lee took me to the back of the house and pointed to an oak tree that had been there a long time. It was spring and the tree was losing its leaves and when you cracked a part of the limb it acted as if the wood was dry and not green. I realized and so did Lee that God had sent him a message through this tree. The tree died and we had to cut it down. It was too close to the house. Lee felt the Lord had told him that he would not live by the representation of the dead tree.

Unforgiveness in my Heart

MARY, A FRIEND I ONCE CARPOOLED TO SCHOOL WITH, was a lady that I held unforgiveness towards her. I asked the Lord to bring her across my path and allow me to ask her for forgiveness. She was a teacher in the High School next door to my Elementary School. The next day we had a meeting with the High School and our school and she sits down beside me in the Auditorium. I tell the Lord, "That was awful soon to meet with her." I have my opportunity to ask and we talk for about 5 minutes then I asked her to forgive me for holding unforgiveness in my soul. She says she doesn't know what I am talking about. I refresh her memory and tell her to please forgive me and she says, "OK." She never knew I held it. God was teaching me that holding on just hurts the one holding it. I was the one holding it and I was released from those feelings. Thank you, Jesus, for that valuable lesson.

Lee's Faith and Last days on this Earth

Three years later Lee calls for the greatest and deeply anointed men in the church to come out and pray for him. I call his brother and I call my mom and she gets her pastor to come too. They arrive and they place him in a chair and surround him with powerful prayers sent up to Heaven. They ask God to supernaturally heal Lee. They are very strong men in the Lord. Lee is no longer on milk. He believes in healing. He knows God and he is serving him and praying to him and finding peace in whatever the Lord does and doesn't do. Praise the Lord for a believing man.

A few days later I was in the swing on my front porch. I told the Lord that if Lee was ready to go to heaven then he could take him home. I also said, "Lord, If he is not ready then please don't allow him to go. Please make sure he is ready and help me to get him ready. I will help in any way you ask me." This happened in June. He had been in so much pain my heart ached for him. He had no quality of life.

Lee's last night at our home was a night that I will remember forever. It was July 5, 2007 and I am in bed solidly asleep. He grabbed me and said, "Pray for me. I am in a lot of pain." I agree to pray for him. I am a hard sleeper and I heard the Lord say, "Get up, he is about to kill himself." I immediately got up and headed up to the front room. He was in his recliner with his hands on his head. I put my hands- on Lee and said, "Devil, take your hands off him. He belongs to Jesus. Go back to Hell where you came from. I rebuke you, Satan. Leave him alone. In Jesus name." I Then prayed that God would lessen the pain and help him. I prayed for the pain to go. The next hour we went to the hospital. He never came home again. My son told me he had a loaded gun up in a cabinet in the kitchen. Thank you Lord for the way you protected Lee from his own hands.

Lee went to the hospital and on the way, he asked me if I would be ok if he had to die. I said, "Yes, I will be fine. I have my God and my son." My son was in college and commuted to USC. He then went on to tell me about that man who had given him acid to drink (1st time I heard this). He contributed to the pain that he had endured. That evil man had helped Lee get worst and had helped put him in the grave. Lee asked me to forgive him for the things he had done. I told him I loved him and I understood what he was going through. I would be there for him all the way to his death.

He entered the hospital and they found his blood pressure was way down. They conducted tests and put him in the hospital. The doctor came to me and told me that he was dying, and they would make him as comfortable as they could. I said, "OK I will call his family and my family to let them know." Lee had a bunch of visitors and they were very concerned but knew he was saved. The Lord prompted me to pray with Lee the sinner's prayer. I asked him to repeat after me, "Lord Jesus, come into my life and forgive me of my sins. I ask you to take my life and make it yours. I know you died on the cross for me and I know you rose again and are seated in Heaven. You are my Savior and I give my heart to you for now and forever more. In Jesus name, I pray." He had been on oxygen and he wasn't as coherent as he should be. So, the

Lord prompted me a few days later to take him through the sinner's prayer a second time and he repeated the words behind me and I said, "Believe it in your heart with all your soul and spirit." He repeated it and I felt he was ready to see my Jesus.

The hospital put him in intensive care and he continued to go down. The little nurse told me that I was so calm and so at peace. She said, "Most people would be crying and tore up about their loved one but you were so calm and not hurting." I told her, "He was going to a place where there is no pain and no tears and Jesus will rock him in his loving arms and welcome him home to Heaven. I knew he was going there and why should I feel bad when he will be in a better place." She said that my faith is very deep. I said, "Yes, it is." She was moved by my deepness of faith in Jesus.

On Sunday July 15, 2007 Lee had his last day on this earth. He had a bad time sleeping because of a lady moaning a lot at night. He was in a good mood and I was talking about me getting him a grave site on Monday from a lady that was moving out of the state. It was in the cemetery he had looked at when he was still at home. He liked it and told me to put him there. Mom and my sister had told me that they would be up at the hospital after church. I looked out the hospital room window and saw them in the parking lot at 9:30 in the morning. My sister told me she had rode her bike that morning and smelled death, and went and told mom they better get up to the hospital and skip church. She would be right because he was very close to death. My brother and his children came and visited Lee. At 5:00 my brother's daughter had a text message come on her phone that said, "When I heard them I answered them." This is scripture from the Bible. At 5:30 we all went to get some food to eat. I waved good-bye to Lee and said, "I love you". He said, "I love you." That was the last time I spoke to him.

When we got back he was asleep and around 7:45 he started taking breaths that kept getting wider and wider apart. His brother, my sister, my mom, and me were with him when he took his last breath and at 7:50 he was gone. All present smelt a sweet aroma in the room as he took his last breath. It was a smell that I had never before witnessed. All of us smelt it. The angels took Lee out of the window and into heaven where there is no pain. He had a very peaceful death. I had told the Lord I did not want Lee to be by himself when he took him home. I wanted to be with him and I was. Lee is in a better place and he will always be healthy and young. Praise the Lord!

THE LETTER

I RECEIVED A LETTER FROM A FELLOW TEACHER AND SHE really made my day. She had been present at the hospital, a lot of the time in those last days Lee was on this earth. She watched me and loved the way I handled his death. I have attached the letter.

Dear Beth,

I am so sorry that I wasn't able to attend Lee's funeral. I was unable to get a babysitter for the children. I know you will understand. I just wanted to write you a letter and express how much I am inspired by your faith, strength, and courage during this time. You simply amaze me. I know Lee was so happy to have someone like you to be there for him, to lead him down the path of salvation and in his time of health and sickness. I was in such awe of you and your family that I have decided to rededicate my life to being a true Christian and Christlike in nature. I want what you have. That sense of letting go to God and have him control your life. You are a wonderful example of what being a Christian can do for your life. Even during a difficult time in your life, you were able to touch others for Christ and that's amazing. I am very sad that Lee will not be with you on earth in a healthy body but I am happy for you knowing that he is free of pain and enjoying his rewards in Heaven. You will be in my prayers. Thank you for being an inspiration.

Sincerely, a teacher friend of mine

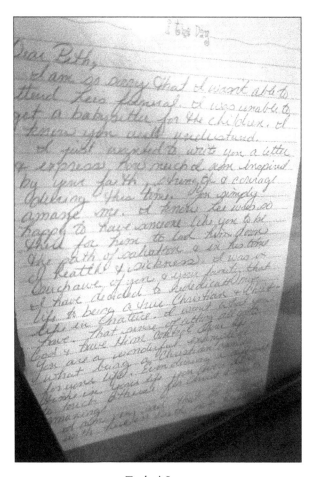

Teacher's Letter

After Lee and my life in the Lord

I CONTINUED TO TEACH FOR 3 MORE YEARS AND TOLD everyone that I was waiting on the Lord to tell me when to stop teaching. That friend who gave me such a sweet letter became a close friend those last few years. I had my son in college and I wanted to keep on working for him as well. He had a scholarship and he kept it those last 2 years and he graduated with a Business degree.

In 2008, I had not one of my azaleas to bloom in my yard. My yard is full of beautiful azaleas and they did not bloom the year after Lee's death. They have bloomed every year since I planted them in the 70's till his death. They have bloomed every year after 08. They were crying over Lee. That is what I summed it up to be.

A few days after Lee died I decided I was going to give the Lord everything that could keep me from loving and serving him. I was giving my God my house and I would need to clean it. My son was away at his girlfriend's house and I saw my opportunity to clean my house and give it to the Lord. I headed down behind my house to the parking lot at the shop. I got a wagon and pulled it down there. It was full of evil tapes that we had from our younger years. I decided I could not give that filth away so I decided to burn it. I asked the Lord how to do this. He said, "Dig a pit." So, I did. Then I said, "What do I use to burn in the pit?" He said, "Use the pinecones you use in the wood stove." So, I got the pinecones and threw them in the pit. I then asked, "What do I need to do if the fire gets out of hand?" He said, "Get the water hose and douse it if you need to." I got the hose and placed it near the pit. I lighted the pit and started piling on the filth that was in those tapes and I burned them until there was no more. As I was burning I saw blue, red, purple, and yellow colors coming from the pile into this colored smoke. I prayed, "Lord don't allow these evil spirits to go into the community but back to hell where they came from." I finished and I had burned everything evil that I felt was in my house. I doused the pit and covered it with dirt and then I lay pine straw on top and you could not tell I had burned anything at all. I went back up to the house and I took a plaque that said ..As for me and my house I will serve the Lord. It had a cross on the plaque and those words. I dedicated my house to the Lord and I danced to him and sang praises to his name. I went to bed and felt my cathedral ceiling had angels fluttering in the ceiling. I felt their presence and knew that I had pleased my God. I was so happy to give up my house and consecrate it clean and right to my God.

The next year I gave my God my 10.68 acres and told him this land was Holy Acres and it belonged to him. I danced with my ipod and praised him for his love and devotion to me. I danced in the azaleas and told him I belong to you and I always will.

The third year I gave him myself. I had bought a cross ring from a jewelry store and I went in the woods behind my house and I lay down on a blanket and I looked up to heaven and praised him with my ipod. It had worship music and I loved and adored him. As I lay there the trees looked as if they were dripping liquid gold. It was so fantastic to see nature joining in worship with me. I looked across into the woods and saw a cross made by 2 trees. It was glowing. I then took the ring and I said, "I marry my soul to you. You are my husband and you are taking Lee's place. I have given you my house, my land, and now me." I placed the ring where my wedding ring had been placed and I became my God's servant. It has 4 's' inscriptions that mean scripture, savior, shepherd, and salvation. I love my Jesus and he is the most important thing to me. I belong to him and I always will. He is my Father and I am his child.

I want to share now a time that I established to meet with my God on January 1st of every year. This was done back when I first met him on the beach. The 1st year I asked the Lord to bring one person across my path to share him with them. On the 2nd year I had 2 people come across my path to share with and I had asked for only one. I said, "You doubled it on me." So, on the 2nd year I asked for 2 people to come across my path. Well the next year I had 4 people to cross my path to share with and he had doubled it again. So, I said to him on the 3rd visit, "I am not giving you a number. Just open my heart and my mouth to share with as many as you desire." I needed his prompting to help me with the people that I share my Jesus with. I said, "You, Lord, take my mouth and help me share my walk with them." Now 30 years later I still have that date in my carport with the Lord. I never have missed this date with the Lord. I also every 2-7, I rededicate my soul to the Lord and remind him that I belong to him. He is mine and I am his.

After Lee's death, I had a new ministry where when an ambulance went by me driving, or by my home or anyplace, I would break out into praying, "If they know you, you can have them. If they do not know you give them a chance to know you because sometimes when they go through a valley they will turn to you. Please Lord have mercy and help them to become believers." I have prayed for thousands of ambulances.

In 2011 my sister and I went to the Endtime Handmaidens and Servants World Convention in St. Louis. We flew out of Charlotte to St. Louis. We had an out of world experience and it was awesome. We had morning and evening meetings and free time in the afternoon. At one of the first meetings we attended my sister saw an angel hovering in the worship. There was a man who carried a cross across the world and he was so humble. Before he spoke he lay face down behind the podium extended on the floor and prayed that the Lord would give him the words to touch us and serve him more. He also said, "The earth is full of the Glory of God." He said that he had been bitten by camels, monkeys, and rats. He said he had been run over by a car. He said that he had been visiting with his cross in a foreign country and was placed in front of a firing squad. They got ready to shoot him and he became so bright they could not see him to shoot him. He blinded them and they couldn't shoot.

Miss Gwen Shaw told of how she died and went to Heaven. The Endtime people prayed her back to earth. She did not want to come back. She was heartbroken. You could tell she had visited and saw her late husband and wanted so much to stay. We also had an airline pilot tell of the heavenly things he saw. He saw George Washington and others in heaven. On our trip, back from Charlotte we found gold dust in the car on the dash. Before I left the Convention, I sent a letter to Miss Gwen and told her about my Lee and how she helped him into the gates of Heaven. I mentioned the prayers sent up in Atlanta by the World. She answered my letter and sent it to my home. It was so special.

My Sister, Donna

After Lee, I started having Bible groups at my school with the school janitorial staff. I had befriended a few ladies in the community too. So, I lead the Bible studies and I brought anointed tapes and shared them with the group. I also shared parts of my life and told them they could have a closer walk with God if they yearned and wanted it more than anything else. He is willing to be your partner in this life. Just get hungry for him. He is very willing. One of the lady's husband was so wayward and far from God. I asked her if she wanted me to send up a powerful prayer. I told her that the heavens responded when that prayer was sent up. She said," Yes." So, we joined hands and prayed, "Lord, whatever it takes, to get him to know you then do it." The next day she told me that he had almost had to go to the doctor. He got real sick. I told her that was a powerful prayer and the heavens move. She realized that it is a powerful prayer. It was prayed over my Lee by my sister because of all the crying I would do over Lee and his unbelief when I visited her in her classroom. After that prayer, he went to the hospital in 2003 for the first time and found the Lord. Heaven moves when it is prayed and God responds.

The year after Lee, I was going to my mom's house for Thanksgiving. I was cooking 2 dishes in the oven to take to her house. I reached in the oven and my back gave out. I had to get my son to take them out for me. All day I could barely walk or move. It was shooting pain like birth pains and oh, how it hurt. At 8pm at my mom's home, mom, my sister, and a holy man on the phone prayed over my back. I was instantly healed. Praise the Lord. No week of pain and I could move like normal. What a Thanksgiving I had because I had to thank my Lord for his touch.

We had Open House at my school in August of 08, and I had a wonderful time talking with my parents. We talked about their child and then I talked about my Lord Jesus. I shared a few of the things I have shared with you the reader and they were so joyful in having a Christian teacher for their child. I had a pastor's kid in my room. I praised him all the way home. I saw after I parked a formation of 2 sticks that made a cross and it was lighted up by the sun in the woods. It glowed and I thanked the Lord for it. I was so happy to be able to share my faith with my parents.

I had learned to trust God after the valley of the Lumina van. I learned to ask before ever buying or deciding anything to do with me and my possessions. I needed another vehicle because my present vehicle was approaching 125k and I wasn't so sure it would last. So, my son and I set out in 08 to find me a new car to drive. I was still teaching and I needed a reliable vehicle. We decided we were going to look at Hondas and Toyotas. I had been looking for 6 months and had not found anything. We drove into the Honda dealership and I parked and told my son, "The search was over." I saw a blue car ahead of us and I wanted it. I had prayed that the Lord would light my eyes up if I found any vehicle that day. My eyes lit up and I wanted that car. It was a Honda Accord. We drove 3 cars and finally the 3rd car was the one I wanted. It was blue (my favorite color) and we came back on Monday and I bought it with cash I had saved for this next vehicle. It was exactly the amount I had saved. Praise the Lord. I still have this car and it has only 29k miles on it. It was a new 08 Honda Accord. It is 9 years old and I have never had a moment's trouble with it. When you let God choose you cannot go wrong. He made us and he knows what we desire.

A year after Lee's death, One of the 1st grade teachers had a husband of many years and he had died. I asked the Lord when I needed to go visit her. He said, "Wait until the 2nd week after his death and then go." I waited and then I set out after school to go visit her. I knew she was an unbeliever. So, I asked him to take control of my mouth and help me to share with her what would be the best stories to tell her. I had been praying for years for her to believe. I had a very nice visit. She was very happy to see me. No one was visiting her but me. I shared my grandmother almost dying and how I promised to take my kids to church if he would spare her life. I then told her how I became a believer. She told me she had enjoyed my stories and I left. I told the Lord that I had said what he brought to mind and I hoped I had planted a seed. As to her faith I have no knowledge if she ever believed. I obeyed.

That weekend I was in my pool laying on my back looking up into the sky. The clouds started rolling overhead and the first thing I saw was a cloud shaped like an angel. Then I saw more angels and I saw Lee's side of his face and he was smiling and I said, "I see you, Lee." He looked so young, healthy, and happy. I looked and saw more angels and then I saw the face of God like we see in books with the white beard. Finally, I saw Jesus on a white horse made up of clouds. I started crying and the tears rolled into my mouth and tasted salty. I immediately went into the house and wrote all that I saw down and thanked the Lord for the visions in the clouds.

A few months later I entered a contest at school for decorating my door at Christmas. The class that won would get a pizza party. I asked the Lord to tell me what I needed to do. He told me to photograph the children looking up like at the sky and singing. He said to make bells above the children and each child made an angel out of a cone and decorated it with red and green glitter. Then they made a bell out of a juice cup and decorated it with lots of glitter and had a jingle bell inside of the cup that rang when the door was moved. The child's photographed face was cut out and placed on the angel's body. I wrote in cutout letters "The angels are singing and the bells are ringing." I won the contest and several teachers asked me where I got the idea and I said, "From the Lord." We had a pizza party and my kids were truly my angels.

A few months later I was out in my chair by the pool and I was looking up into the sky. There wasn't a cloud in the sky. I was praising my Lord and enjoying the pretty day. I looked up as I lay down and I saw a head of Jesus in the sky. He was clear as a crystal. He was no cloud. I started looking at the top of his head. I saw the thorns in his head. My eyes came down and I saw his eyes and they looked sad. My eyes continued down and his robe was wet and sparkling in the sky. I said "Lord why are you so sad and crying so hard"? He said "The world does not know me." I said "I will get busy and work for you and make you happy. I love you and I want to make you happy. I don't like to see you so unhappy." I got to work and shared him, as much as I had him prompting me to do it. He will tell me to speak to this person and I would. I am his mouthpiece and I will never stop sharing him as long as I live.

THE LORD CALLS ME OFF MY JOB AND THE JUDGMENT HOUSE

THE NEXT YEAR IN MAY, MY SON WAS GETTING MARRIED and he was having a housewarming and I went to the event. At the event a lot of her (his fiancé's) family, were teachers like me. They asked me when I was going to retire from teaching. I had 36 years in first grade. I told them, "When the Lord calls me off my job I will quit but not until he speaks." The next day was Sunday and I went to church and came home and decided to go outside and walk around the pool. All of a sudden the Lord speaks, "I want you to quit your job and serve me 24/7. Your heart is very ripe for me." I said "Lord, I have one question to ask you. "Will I regret this because you know how much I love teaching?" He said, "Never a day will you regret this decision." I said "OK, Lord. I will retire from teaching." The little bird in the tree beside me was screaming, "Purty, Purty." The next day I returned to school and I sent a message to my Principal that I needed to see her as soon as possible. She sent someone to my classroom and I headed to her office. I told her that the Lord had called me off my job and I was to serve him 24/7. So, I was quitting my job and I would be retiring in June. I gave my resignation to her the very next day. God had called me off my job and I was obeying him and I would work for him. That was a day I will never forget and by the way

85

I have never regretted my decision to obey.....not one day have I regretted the decision even to this day.

Me on my last day of school 2010

My children my last year of teaching were one of the sweetest groups I ever taught. I would like you to see some of their letters to me that last year. I treasure them because they were the apple of my eye. These children and their parents tried to get me to stay and I told them that the Lord had called me off my job. They were the only thing that could have changed my mind. I only miss the children. They were the inspiration that I had for teaching. 7

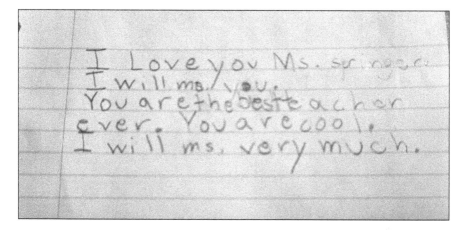

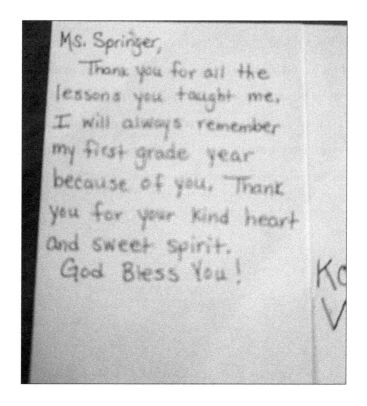

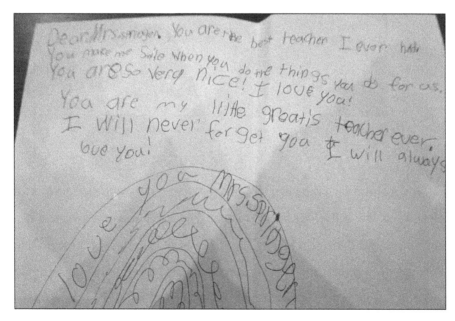

My letters from my children to me on my last day teaching 2010

My mom, sister, granddaughter, and me went to a church (they did this for Halloween) that had a Judgement House in the Church where you visited each site and watched the people playacting. We went by a total of 5 scenes and then we went in this dark place (mom and granddaughter did not). A group of young teenage girls went in with my sister and me. When the demons came out of the darkness the young girls were so afraid they pushed to get out. They bum-rushed the door and almost knocked my sister down. I helped her, and we later saw these girls get saved after this event. After this we went to visit Heaven. It was awesome place to be. Such peace and love and I felt so loved. As we left a young lady in the parking lot was sobbing. My mom went over to her and took her hand and asked if she could pray for her. She agreed and I saw my mom's faith at work. She always cares for others and recognizes a need when it comes across her path. I asked the Lord to make me more like her, and open my eyes to times I can reach out to others. Take away my spiritual blindness to other's needs.

A few months later my brother had health problems and he had surgery to correct it. At first our family thought it was a terrible diagnosis. We were scared it was going to threaten his life. I asked the Lord why was this happening to him. He told me that he was taking him into a valley to draw him closer to him. I got the opportunity to share this info with my brother at my sister's house a few days later. He cried at the revelation. My brother is a UPS driver and he meets a lot of people on his route. He is fine today and serves our God.

My sister, my brother, and me 2010

The Lord's Ways

GOD HAS 3 DIFFERENT TIMES TOLD ME HE IS COMING back soon. I told you the reader about the 1ˢᵗ time and I will tell about the last time. My son and I ate at Waffle House and we returned home. When I arrived home about an hour later my stomach was running off and I stayed in the bathroom. I had eaten chili and it tore up my stomach. The Lord after about 2 hours called me to his presence. I visit him in my closet and I went and said "Lord I have a bad stomach." He told me it would not bother me again. I went in the closet and waited to hear from him. It took about 10 minutes before he spoke. He said "I am coming back soon. Get busy." I told him I would and thank you for your message. I believe in the Rapture and I feel that any day Jesus can come and take us to heaven. We will fly through the air in the wink of an eye. I can't wait to be in the presence of my Savior.

I have had 2 out of body experiences. One time I was on the internet singing with Franklin Graham and he was so anointed that I left my body for one hour. I landed back in my body and I looked around the room to determine where I was. I also had one when I was relaxing in a chair outside by the pool and I was gone for about 1 hour again. I landed back in my body and wondered where I was. While I was gone I do not remember that part. But I felt so anointed when I returned to my body. I know that I was gone.

The clock told me that I had been gone both times. Praise to God and he is so Good. I love him.

I was asking the Lord for another husband. I told him that this man had to be a Christian. I did not want to go through an unbelieving husband. I had been there and done that. He told me that the 3rd man would be the one. I dated a man and he was so into himself that he did not even hardly talk but listen to music. My 2nd date this man was into me but he had been married 5 times and I did not want to be number 6. He called me and asked for another date and I said, "No." The 3rd man had blue eyes and he was congenial and loved the fact that I was a Christian. He called me for a 2nd date and I told him we were going to have a Bible study and he was to bring his Bible. We met at a park in my town and he brought his Bible and we had a Bible study. His Bible was very worn and used profusely. We had a very good Bible study and he pretty well knew the Bible. We also prayed and joined hands and asked God to help us serve him in every way we could. This man became my 2nd husband within 13 months of meeting. He has a house in the northern part of our state. I had my water to go out (have a pump) and we went up to his house and he gave me his master suite as my room. We had a nice time and he seemed to be the one. He called me beautiful.

The day after I met Barry, my next -door neighbor had her husband to die and I went to pay my respects to her. I had just dated the 3rd fellow the day before and I went and shared my Jesus with them and I told them some of the stories I share with others. The lady told me I was good therapy for her after losing her husband. We were laughing at some of the events that we had shared and it was fun. She is a very deep Christian and walks very close to my God. This is the home that the robbery took place earlier in my book.

On March 31, 2012, Barry (my 2nd husband) and I were married down at mom's pond, and it was a beautiful wedding. We had a pastor from down there to marry us, and we both after the ceremony had a chance to pray over our marriage. We made the Lord Jesus number one in our lives. We loved each other and we had a honeymoon down at Siesta Beach in Florida. It was a beautiful beach and so nice to visit. I had never visited there before. We visited a church down there and they were so nice and loving towards us. On the way, back we visited a church that Barry had attended when he lived in Jacksonville, Florida. When we travel we always make it a point to go to church wherever we roam.

Barry and I on our Wedding day

94

For our Wedding gift to each other I asked Barry to write me a letter and tell me what he was feeling about our union. Here is his letter and it truly touched me.

My darling Beth,

I have not written a Love letter before so I will try to put words on paper that seem to come so easily from my mouth. Love is the willingness to extend one's self, for the purpose of nurturing one's own and another's "spiritual growth", looking to meet other kindred spirits, someone who knows the difference between self- love and self- absorption. Someone who doesn't wear their arrogance as if it were a badge of honor. They have no tolerance for abuse or deception. One day I smiled and found the warmth of my smile reflected back to me. One day I reached out to someone and found I only had to reach halfway because you were reaching out to me. One day I reached out and found the meaning of the word "love" that many use so carelessly. One day I found someone with whom I can share and now I try to know myself and the world around me and now the time is here for me to give you my heart. I love you with a very "personal Love" that comes from so deep within. A very respectful love for my Lord tells me to love you as he loves the church. His church that is within us. My love for you is such that when we are apart I feel as though a part of me is missing. I knew when our hands touched, you were very special and I knew then I was in love with you. Yes, "sweetheart" I felt it then and haven't stopped yet. I try to tell you and let you know constantly you are the love of my life for now and forever more. I have but one heart and you have captured it totally, my Love. As I said before I don't know any fancy word only 3 that matter, "I love you." Till God calls us home. .....Me."

Barry and I on our Honeymoon in Siesta beach in Florida, 2012

My Lee had a john boat in the shop that I never needed or used after his death. We used it a lot in fishing all over this state. I decided to sell it and I did not know what was a fair price. I asked the Lord to show me. One day I was in the front yard singing to my God. All of a sudden 6 little guinea pigs walked in a line through my front yard winding through the azaleas. I have never seen guinea pigs ever in my yard. I knew it was a sign from the Lord. I said "Lord 6k is fair price for the boat. Thank you." A retired policeman bought the boat and after buying it gave me a bunch of fish to eat that he caught. God will help you if you make him the captain of your life. Hand your life over to him, and he is there at all times.

I have a driveway that turns into a rip-rap that jars you around in your vehicle. My first husband used our tractor to get the driveway level. So, my Barry tells me that we need to get it paved. I said, "Yes, we do." We have a company to come and I think pave it but in reality, I got nothing but rocks and rocks and they are under my nice carport. I am distraught and miserable. I cry out to my God and say, "I did not want a rock pile." I cried and I cried and finally he spoke. He said 4 little words that made me happy. He said "It can be fixed." Barry and I go to his house and I call some people that paved his driveway and I get no answer. The second day we are up there a man catches my husband by the mailbox and asks him if he knew any one that needed a driveway paved. My husband said, "Yes, my wife needs hers paved." My husband's house is way back in the country. There is no way that at that moment he was at the mailbox and the very person I needed came up. It was my God and only him. The next week my rock pile was paved smoothly and I was one happy lady. Praise you Lord.

A few months later I went on a hunt with my camera for nature's crosses. I looked at my husband's house and found beautiful crosses and I took a picture of them. I found more than 20 because he is in the country and it is so beautiful up there. I found crosses by looking at roses, shadows, sticks, trees, and vines. I found one that was leaning and the Lord told me that it was like the cross his son bore for us. Then I went on a hunt at my house. I found just as many on my place as his. They are formed by vines or trees crossing each other to form a cross in nature. I shared my pictures in my Sunday school class and they were amazed at the Glory of God in nature. You can find them if you turn on your spiritual eyes and they will appear.

Crosses I found in nature 2011

I spend a lot of time at my husband's home singing on my ipod to my Jesus. He is worthy of our praise and we should never neglect this part of our walk with him. I also spend a lot of time worshipping my Lord in my azaleas.

My ipod has songs that I sing directly to him. For ex. (I love you. You are my king. I adore you). I believe this brings you closer to our Savior.

Me today 2015

There was a day I was at my house and Barry was at his house. I was cleaning out a desk in my bedroom that contained a lot of cards and things I had kept that people and family had sent me. I came across a beautiful card that was from Lee and I found a card from me to Lee on our 19ᵗʰ Anniversary. We had given each other the exact card. I cried and cried over the fact that we were so close and had the same minds were present at that place in time. His words really warmed my heart and I felt his love through that card. It brought back the memory in Charleston the summer of 06 when we went to the Holiday Inn that sits on a piece of land that is surrounded by water and is shaped like a cylinder. I stepped out on the balcony and my God spoke. He said that this would be the last vacation I would ever spend with Lee. It was the last vacation we ever had together. I realized that Lee was getting very close to Heaven. We visited the Classic car place in Summerville and drove over the new suspension bridge. We enjoyed our last special time together. It brought back those precious memories and I really cried. I missed Lee and knew he was in a better place and one day I will see him again.

The Power Team, Amish Country, and the Wreck

Every summer my church (Christian Life) has some guys come who we call the Power team and they share the word like a revival and people get slain in the Spirit. I have been up many times and the men come toward me and I collapse on the floor with the Lord. He speaks to me and tells me he is filling me with his gifts. I am so drunk I cannot walk for hours. I speak in other languages and I get filled with what my Lord feels I need. They visit our church for 4 days in September and a lot of the people get slain. I love the touch of my Savior and every year I am present. Barry goes with me and sometimes my sister or my mom. All of my family are slain as well. We are a Christian family who places our lives in our Savior's hands. I started going to this church after Lee's death. It is where I attend today.

One Sunday night we had the African Children's Choir to perform in my church. They danced with all their little innocent hearts and sang like angels. They really made me think about how our American children are so mature (not in a good way) and have lost their innocence and become so worldly. They never have the shining hope that I saw displayed on the sweet little African children's faces. They really moved their little bodies in a cute and innocent way. They come from poverty and with little hope of a better life.

This is a way out of poverty and the future shines all over those precious children's faces. They are so precious and lovely. I really was impressed.

A year later Barry and I visited the Amish community in Ohio. We enjoy the simple lifestyle they live. They are very loving and caring people that love the Lord. We saw many carriages and horses and many bikes. We went to the cheese factory that the Amish run and bought some cheese. As we were checking out Barry handed the cashier the money and over paid by 20$ and she immediately said he had handed her too much money. She gave it back to Barry and I was very impressed by their honesty. They live the walk and talk the walk with my God.

Amish Country 2012

A few weeks later Barry and I were headed to Florida to purchase a car and we were in a wreck with a truck who made a u turn right in front of us as we were traveling the road. He had a stop sign and he pulled out in front of Barry and I and we totaled his car. The air bags went off and I saw it imploding and my mind didn't process that I was in a wreck. God kept us safe inside that Avalon. The paramedics arrived and looked me over and said, "You will live with this pain the rest of your life". I said, "I do not claim that and I serve a powerful God and he keeps me safe." God preserved us and we both were fine after this wreck. Barry wanted to sue them but I had no idea I would because it did not cost me even 50$. I went to the Doctor and he found nothing wrong with me. Barry sustained some teeth damage because of the air bag hitting him in the face. I asked the Lord why this happened. He told me that I was there to show my faith to the paramedics and the 1st responders and that is exactly what I did. One of the fireman was a cousin to a child I had taught years ago. The child I taught was away at Clemson and grown up getting ready to graduate. What a small world we live in.

LIVING FOR MY LORD AND SERVING HIM

THAT WINTER I NEEDED MY CHIMNEY CLEANED SO I HAD called a man and he was coming out to clean my chimney. I had a wood stove that had been in my home since it was built. It was permanently installed and you had to clean it from the roof and through the stove. He entered my house in a bad mood. He was fussing about the last place he had been. He looked at my wood stove and put a cloth down on the floor and began to pull it out of the brick wall. It did not give. He looked at me and said, "I can't clean this. It is illegal to have a stove like this." I said, "ok." He looked at me and said," Why are you so calm? I can't clean this and yet you didn't get upset with me." I said, "I am a deep Christian and if one door closes another will open." He said, "That explains it. I see you are not upset with me. You are something else." I said, "God bless you, sir and thank you for trying." I got my son to do it for me the next weekend. God is in control of our lives and he brings people across our path to show others the way to go and to act.

A few months later I was returning from Barry's home and I was traveling on I77 and I had a trailer behind my Tahoe and I was going back to my house to put the trailer up and stay there till Barry arrived. I had pieces of plywood in the bottom of the trailer wired in there as a floor for the trailer. One piece flew up and landed on the back ramp that formed the back of the trailer. I was afraid it would come loose and fly up into someone's windshield and so I slowed down and got off on the shoulder of the interstate and came to a stop. The plywood fell into the trailer and I tried to put it in the Tahoe but it would not fit. I left it at that place and decided to merge but I could not get back on the interstate because the traffic in the right lane was back to back. I asked the Lord what should I do. He told me to go to the next exit and get up my speed and merge with the oncoming traffic. So, I did and it worked so much better. Thank you, Lord. Barry arrived at my house and we had a nice time together. We were watching tv and some bad language came on the tv and he changes the channel. We are Christians who monitor the tv and if it offers ugly language or blaspheming my God we change the channel. I remember with Lee I had to leave the room. I am so happy to be with a Christian.

A few days later Mom called me when she was going through chemotherapy and told me this testimony. She was praising the Lord and getting close to him. It was a Sunday and he, Jesus, came into the room and put a blanket over her. He said he was healing her and it was the oil of healing over her. She also had a dream and was worried about no hair and he showed her a vision of how she looked to him. He showed her a lovely woman with beautiful black hair. She was touched by this vision and did not worry again. He brought her peace and healing in every way.

A month later I was at Barry's house and I was on his front porch (it goes the whole length of his house). I was praising my God in Heaven and he spoke and said, "This is like my throne room." I was amazed at his words. I was also on that same porch and I was dancing and singing to my God on another day and I got a nail in my foot. It was bleeding and I got it to stop. I asked the Lord how did I find one nail in that big porch and get it in my toe.

He said, "Magnify the pain by 1000x and that is the intensity of the pain I endured for you on the cross." I said, "OK, Lord, I humble myself. It doesn't hurt not in relation to your pain." Then the same day I got bit by a wasp on the back porch. I had a 3- ingredient sting medicine that I put on the sting and it vanished. That 3- ingredient medicine for bee, wasp, or yellow jacket's stings is as follows: 1 cup of household ammonia, 1 tp. Baking soda, and 1 tp. Meat tenderizer. Mix the 3 together and rub on your skin after a sting and it vanishes (the pain). I got this recipe for stings from a lady that helped me in my 1st grade classroom. Before we were mandated to not put anything on a child we put this on screaming kids and they stopped immediately upon placing this on the sting. It truly works. Barry drove his lawnmower up at his house into a nest of yellow jackets and they attacked him by biting him all up. He wanted me to get that 3- ingredient potion and put it on the stings. I did and he was fine and the whelps went down and the sting was gone. Try it and you will like it.

Barry's Times

A YEAR AFTER WE WERE MARRIED, BARRY AND I WAS AT the beach and having a beautiful time picking up shells. We got near the place I met the Lord for the 1st time and saw the butterflies and a dolphin jumped 5 feet in the air right where I met my God. It was so special because my life changed and I chased after my God as a fireball for him right after my experience of those butterflies. He was letting me know that that place is so special and I will encounter other things in the future. He is so good to those who love and serve him.

Barry's President of his bank was a personal friend of his. He visited with her a few weeks later and she and he had a close bond. One day I was present when she was telling Barry how much she was worried about her husband in Iraq and his safety. She has 2 small children she is raising while he is deployed. My heart went out to her and when Barry and I came back to his house I went to my closet (my intercessory closet) and prayed deeply and with intercessory prayers over her and her family. I petitioned God to have mercy on her and help her in every way he could. He spoke and said that the husband of the Bank President would never go and be deployed again. He would be there to help raise those children and be there for his wife. I was overjoyed to hear those words of comfort. A few months later the Lord told me to tell her what he had said. I told her and she said, "He had retired and wasn't going again." Wow the Lord was right.

A few days later I was at my house reading my Bible. I looked at the word and It came ALIVE on the page and I realized that the word is living and we can gain a lot by being in it every day. If I miss a day from the word I feel as if I am starving for the food it brings me. It was perfect understanding and after this I had bronchitis and I was severely sick. After this illness, I quit drinking sweet tea and wanted nothing but water. The Lord healed me and I was fine but had left my tea fix cold turkey. I drank tea since I was a little girl. Today I drink water at all times. God can take away your desire for things that are not good for you.

For Christmas that year I wanted a picture of my Jesus and Barry and I went to the Christian book store and found the picture I wanted. They told us to wait for the picture for 2 weeks and then check back then. We had picked it out of a newspaper, around Thanksgiving and ordered it then. So, in 2 weeks we came and asked about the picture. It was on reorder and we would have to wait another week. Barry wanted it for a Christmas gift from him to me. So, with one week left and no picture in sight I looked around the store and found one that I wanted in the place of the one we had ordered. It was a lot more expensive and it would do. They let Barry get that picture for 5$ more than the one ordered which was a lot smaller and not as nice as this one. God brought me a 150$ picture for 50$. Praise the Lord. I told Jesus that he looked Jewish in that picture. This picture is the picture that the children who visited Heaven say Jesus looks to them. I have it in my living room across from my chair I sit in most of the time.

Me at my house today 2015

Barry is a very giving man. He meets a lot of needs by giving money and his time to others. He has taught me to be more giving to the needy when they have needs. When the Lord prompts me to give to an individual I will obey. A man in our Sunday school class stood up and said he was broke. His wife had recently died. I gave to this man and so did Barry. A lady in my community called Barry and asked him to help her get her a well drilled for she had no water. He paid for the drilling and she had a new well. This same lady was losing her home to foreclosure and he once again payed for her house to be saved. Barry is a very giving and lovely man of the Lord. A lady needed a refrigerator and he gives her the refrigerator that is in his kitchen. Wow so giving and truly living the word of God.

We took our Sunday School teacher and his wife up to Barry's house to spend the night with us before the Sunday school teacher had to preach in a church in the upstate. His wife gave a testimony about how she became a Christian. She was a little girl around 4 years of age with an older sister. They begged their mom to let them go to the church at the end of the row of mill houses. She finally allowed them to go up the street and into the church while she watched. They went for about 1 or 2 months. Then they shared with mom what they had learned so she went with them a few times and got saved and so did their dad. From then on, they lived there and went to church and their home became a Christian home. The Lord can use children to help adults to believe. Awesome the way our Father provides faith in such a lovely way. We enjoyed our time together and prayed together as a group before they left the next morning.

On a Saturday morning Barry and I are going to his house and the phone rings. It is my sister screaming and hollering and crying. I kept telling her to calm down and tell me what is going on. I gathered that mom had hit her head and it was bleeding and she was incoherent. Barry and I went to the Hospital and sat outside and watched for the ambulances rolling in to see the one from my mom's community. I was praying for her to be ok. Then her ambulance arrived and I walked over to see her and recognized her shoes sticking out of the blanket. Her head was covered with things to keep her from bleeding. When they wheeled her out and I saw her face, she looked like the "Passion of Christ" image with that bleeding head. She said, "I'll be ok." I asked the paramedics if she was ok and they said that she will be fine. I went back and waited on my sister. She arrived and was crying profusely. She told me that they were pulling a large tree branch out of a tree behind the pickup truck with a chain and the branch swung and hit mom and her dog. Mom said that it was coming for her and she grabbed her dog to get out of the way. My sister said that mom was face down in the leaves and not breathing. My sister turned her head to help her breathe. The dog was licking her. The dog was killed and mom was severely injured. They had to put 20 staples in her head to stop the bleeding and she had a hairline fracture in her collarbone. Her hand and foot were swollen too. My sister said she had a dream of mom standing in front of a grill and the grill flared up with fire in front of her face. She had this dream the night before the incident. Mom stayed for a week with me and I changed her bandages and took care of her. My sister is a teacher and she had to go to school. I prayed that the Lord would give them wisdom about moving tree branches and allowing others to do that. It is too dangerous to be doing this by themselves. Remember the branch killed her dog. God is so good. Sometimes the event takes you by surprise and prayer is sometimes hard to come by. I found this to be true when this was going down.

I paid for my Sin

A FEW WEEKS LATER I HAD BEEN UP AT BARRY'S HOME and I had been praising the Lord and I got into some sumac and I broke out itching all over my body. I had it really bad on the top of my face. I went to my doctor and he put me on steroids. It spread all over me and I had a time sleeping at night because of the bumps itching and my scratching. Barry coated the bumps with a topical solution for itching and that helped some. He is a very caring man that helps in any way he can. This went on for 2 weeks and I seemed to get worse. I praised my God on my ipod and I cried out to him from the depths of my soul. I told him to have mercy on me. I love you and I know you can heal me of this blood and skin disease. I cried and I cried big crocodile tears over my body. I told him it makes me itch, I scratch and bumps break out, and then my skin turns to leather. It feels like ants are biting me and it is all over my torso, legs, arms, fingers, and face…..my whole body. He heard my cries for help and he said words I wanted so much to hear. He said, "Look". I saw a cross glowing across the road from Barry's porch made by 2 tree limbs in a cross configuration. Then he spoke again and said, "I will heal thee." He did and he made every bump disappear and my skin was restored to its rightful place. I danced and praised him and I fell in love deeply with my precious Savior. He is my help in times of need. Praise you my Jesus. This is my words to him……"You healed me and supernaturally healed every bump. Thank you, my Savior. You are so thoughtful and caring. I am your child and you heard me cry out in agony. Help me Lord not to sin against you and make me pure and holy in thy sight. I will always be yours and I will serve you all the days of my life on this earth. In Jesus name, I pray." This was the result of some sin I had in my life. God will punish you for them, and I had to pay the price for my sin. Try to be holy and try to not sin. We are only human and it happens to the deepest servants of God. He will help you not to sin. Just ask him. He is ready and willing to assist you as his child.

Me today 2016

Working to Help the Lord

At one of the Power Team visits I met a little lady that kept eyeing me and was sitting right next to me so, I struck up a conversation with her and she told me she had been married 23 years and her husband left her and the children for another woman. She was hurt so bad that she thought of ending it 2 weeks ago. I said to her, "That was the lie of the Devil. Don't go there. Get Jesus and he will comfort you and make it a lot easier if you let him have the hurt. He can pull you through and make life a lot better." I asked if I could pray for her and so we joined hands and prayed together that God would help her and give her peace that surpasseth understanding. I have been friends with her ever since that day. Every Power Team we have she is there. God protected her and brought her through the deep valley she had to traverse. He will do it for you too. Just ask and he will be eager to rush to your side.

Barry had a dually that could not be washed by car washes so we went to a car wash that hand washed his truck. I waited inside and he watched the washing of his truck. A young man sat down beside me and we struck up a conversation. He said I looked like I was in my 30's and I was in my 50's. I told him I had taught 1st grade 36 years. He said, "How did you stay so young looking?" I said, "No stress, love what you do for a living, and being a Christian." I told him about the butterflies at the beach and he said what I had told him was inspirational. It really touched him by my testimony. This is why I visit the parking lot every new year to help me say the right things to the people I meet across my path. God takes my mouth and I say whatever he prompts me to say. This is a lifestyle that I have adopted to be my mantra. I want to share him every chance I get.

A month later Barry and I went on a dinner trip with his neighbors across the road. They told us there was a lady in their church who had been burnt out. So, we got up the items she was in need of and gave them to the neighbors we had talked to. The neighbors said we did not know this lady but yet we were willing to help. I told her that the Bible told us to do this. When there is a need we will rise to the occasion. She was in awe of our generosity. Barry and I help others and we might not know them. Yet God prompts us to do this for him and to wake up those who do not do this. We trust in our God.

A month later my mom had to go to the Hospital in my city to have a bone biopsy. Barry and I went with her. It was a wonderful experience for mom. She was at peace and very calm and she had a" Holy" time. She shared with her little unmarried pretty nurse about my dad and his Heaven experience and about other times the Lord worked in her life. I shared my butterflies story at the beach. She was in awe of our testimonies. Then mom's Pastor came in to see her and pray for her. He prayed for mom, all the patients in the hospital, and the doctors and nurses. Then he gave his testimony of his wife and the cancer that had a hold on her. He told about the doctors and nurses giving him no hope and they said they had done all they could do for his wife. She lit up the screen with cancer spread almost all over her body. So, the Pastor told the Lord, "Why is the verdict so grim, Lord? You can heal her. Please Lord." He pleaded with the Lord and the Lord said, "Who do you choose to believe, me or the doctors?" He said, "You Lord, I believe you can heal her." Six weeks later they tell him she is cancer free. His testimony was awesome and Barry noticed that all the nurses and doctors and patients heard the words of the Pastor. They were listening in to hear him. While they were sticking mom, I stepped out and a little young lady and I struck up a conversation. I told her about the Lord taking me off my job. She said, "A lot of people don't think God speaks." I said, "Yes, I know." She said, "I know he speaks. I have heard him." I said, "That's right, honey." When it was time to leave mom grabbed that little unmarried nurse's hand and prayed with her. Mom prayed that the little nurse would find a Christian young man to marry and have a family with. She also prayed that the little nurse would be a light for the others around her.

Barry and I were at his bank in Rock Hill and I sat down and waited on him and struck up a conversation with an elderly lady. I asked her how she liked the snow. She said she waited inside for it to go. I told her I had been a 1st grade teacher for 36 years and how the Lord called me off my job. I told her how he had reassured me I would never regret it and I haven't. I told about the little bird screaming, "Purty, Purty," as he spoke to me. Then she said I want to tell you something and she said, "I taught 1st grade 30 years like you. I loved it and did not want to quit." I was amazed that I had found a teacher that had loved 1st graders just like me. So, it was so good. I talked to her about many things to do with teaching and we had like minds.

At church one Sunday a few weeks later, a young girl asked me if I was teaching. I told her I wasn't teaching because the Lord called me off my job. I told her that it was in 2010 with 36 years. I said that the Lord said my heart was ripe for him and I was to retire and I asked him if I would live to regret it and he reassured me that I would not regret this decision. I have not missed it either just as he told me. She told me that my words were an inspiration to her. I am my Lord's mouthpiece and I am ready every time he prompts me to share with others.

A year later we had a Father's Day at our church. I noticed a man who had lost his wife 9 months ago and he is really missing her. My heart ached for him and I told Barry we need to take him out for lunch and foot the bill on this Father's Day. Maybe we can cheer him up and get his mind off his deceased wife's passing. We asked him at Sunday School class to go with us and we would meet him there. He came and we really had him laughing and happy and we wished him a Happy Father's Day. We are on this earth to help others as they face events that hurt them and still are fresh on their minds.

A few days later one of our Sunday School members was in the Hospital. We saw his wife in our class. We asked how was he doing and could we help. She said they needed money and we helped. After lunch, we visited this man in the Hospital. We were shocked when we saw him. He is a very deep Christian man and he cares deeply for his family. He was upset because the hospital thought he was drunk and that is why he stepped out in front of a vehicle and was thrown to the ground in pain. The ambulance arrived and the girl paramedic asked him what he was drinking or what drugs was he on. They slammed him up into the ambulance with a broken leg. They kept pushing and slamming him. He said that it really hurt every time they touched him. The ER doctor asked him what he had been drinking or what kind of drugs was he on. They took his broken leg and twisted it. His care was horrible by these assuming people that did not perform a breathalyzer on him. My heart bled for this man and I knew Barry and I needed to pray for him and that the hospital would do a breathalyzer on him and quit jumping to conclusions that were not true. He was very depressed and Barry and I prayed with him for the truth to come to the forefront. As we stood in the Hospital it brought back memories of Lee and how he died in this Hospital. I also gave him the name of a powerful lawyer in my town. He said that he was labelled the "bad Patient" and he asked for a blanket and they tossed it on his bad leg. Then the nurse jabbed him with her long nails and blood squirted out. They had not done any blood tests or urine tests to verify their lies. I got home and I prayed in my closet for the truth to be told and that this Christian man was not guilty as charged. He was innocent and they were wrong. I have a different opinion of this Hospital. I don't think I will ever darken the doors of this Hospital ever again. They have changed and they are cruel.

Barry carries a card that gives the reader a reason to wonder about their relationship with our Jesus. He says on the card…. you may have met me but if you do not know him you have something to worry about. His name is Jesus,….our Savior. The card has a red cross in the right corner. Barry is friends with a bank cashier and he handed her this card and she told him that she did not know he was that way. She told him she was walking with a Pastor's wife in her community. So, I did my Bible study when we arrived home and I prayed for this little lady to come to know my Lord through whatever means he provides. Barry loves my Lord and tries to help those unbelievers to believe. Thank you, Lord for a man after your own heart.

Barry had a Chart that had all the names of Jesus and the corresponding scripture to back it up. We took it to Michael's to get it framed to put in Barry's house. I have included the list at the end of this book. We met a lady in the children's department and struck up a conversation. She was looking for her grandchild a gift. I told her I had taught 1st grade for many years and I could assist her. We asked her about the Lord Jesus and she said she was a Catholic. I told her about finding my Lord at the beach with the butterflies. She hugged me and told me I had inspired her. We asked if we could pray for her and we joined hands and prayed for her husband to find a job and help her in every way to make this transition easy. They were new in the community. I also prayed for her when I arrived back at Barry's house to make her his, and to bless her and give her a chance to come closer to my Jesus.

I heard this testimony on a tv program and It touched me so much I wrote it down. Here it is as she told it. A lady was walking by a man in the dark and he looked like he was going to attack her. She whispered, "Lord, help me and send your angels to help me." She walked on to her car and was glad he did not attack her. The next day she saw his face on tv and recognized him and went to the police station to help with the case. He had attacked another lady a few minutes after this lady had encountered him. She identified him and pointed him out in a lineup. She asked him why he didn't attack her. He said, "Are you kidding? I would never have attacked you because of the 2 big men on each side of you." She knew then that the Lord had sent those angels to protect her that she had prayed for. Wow, God is there when we call on him.

Barry's stroke and Pastor's Attack

On January 25, 2016, Barry and I were taking my Accord up to his house to have Michelon tires put on the car at Costco. We had a nice talk as we traveled up the interstate. It takes 1 hour and 15 minutes to reach his home. We got out of the car and he was opening the door and he could not seem to line up the key in the lock to unlock the front door. I began to feel that something was going on with him. We went in after 3 minutes of unlocking the door and I went and put my suitcase up in my room. Then I turned around and saw him falling on his right side. He got out of a chair and had a time walking. I asked him what was going on and he opened his mouth and nothing came out. He could not speak and he was falling around. He wobbled down the hall and turned to turn on the air and he collapsed on the floor as if his right side was paralyzed. I helped him up and put him in a chair and told him I thought he was having a stroke. I called 911 and had to keep him in the chair. They arrived and said he had a stroke on his left side which controls the right side. They took him to a helicopter and airlifted him to a Charlotte Hospital that dealt with stroke victims. I was told by the paramedics to go to a Hospital in the middle of Charlotte. I drove my car and met him at the Hospital. I called his son and let him know about the stroke. They took me back to see him and he was very paralyzed on his right side. His arm, mouth and leg were with no feeling. They put him in ICU and I spent the night with him. I told the Lord that if he died I didn't want him to be by himself.

The family arrived and they were so supportive. That night he tried to take the probes off his chest with the left hand and a little nurse did not know what to do. The nurse that watched Barry nonstop came in and told the little nurse that I know what to do. She took a soft mitt and put that left hand in it and fastened it to the side of the bed. He never touched the probes again. All night she had a gentle and comforting voice that he responded to very nicely. She really impressed me. I loved the bedside voice that she used with him and knew how to calm him down. As the night progressed, I could not sleep but kept my eyes on the monitor across the room. It talked about an award that you could nominate a nurse to receive it. Guess who came to mind. I nominated that little nurse that watched him all night for that Daisy Award. I filled out the forms and she will get a dinner and a present and recognition for a job well done. She had just transferred from another Hospital to this one. The Lord wanted me to honor her for her work and I did. Barry came through the night fine and they put him in a regular room. I was praying for him and for his healing. They said the left side of his brain was blocked from blood and that is what caused the stroke.

I let him hear the music on my ipod and he listened and it helped him to be at ease. I asked the Lord what was going on and he said, "I was on a Journey for him." I said, "Ok, Lord. Take my hand and lead me to help those that don't know you." He progressed better and better each day and I stayed at his house and went to see him over the next 2 weeks.

A few days later I went to the Charlotte Hospital and parked the car in a parking lot that I did not know. I found my way to his room and I read scripture over him. That night (I waited because of the traffic) and went to go to his house after 8pm. I looked for my car and could not find it. I was in garage after garage and I could not find my car. I cried out to my God and all of a sudden, a cop appeared in front of me. He said he would take me to a person who could help me. That person was security and he took me right to my car. I thanked him and left. One day at this hospital his daughter in law told me about the time her mother died. She said that on the day of her death she stood up and said "Jesus" and she just glowed and glowed and fell down dead. What a testimony. I wrote it down.

Barry stayed 2 weeks and then I had him brought down to my area for rehab. They put him in rehab and he was growing weaker and weaker and after a week he was placed in the Hospital beside the rehab. He was going downhill very fast. The doctor in the ER said he was dying. They put him in that Hospital to let him die. I went to my house and I decided to get in the word and get all the healing scriptures that I could muster up. The next day I went to pray the scriptures over him and to pronounce life over him. The Doctor had pronounced death and my God pronounced life. I prayed with all my might to heal him and help him to get better. The Doctor had no idea how he had gotten better. I told him that I had prayed over him and that God had heard my prayer and made him stronger. I said. "God is the reason he lives." God heard my prayer and in 2 weeks he was back in another rehab that let him get better and better at a slower pace. One day in this hospital I was reading a book about Heaven to Barry. A little maid was in the room cleaning the room and she asked me what was the title of the book I was reading. I gave her the book and said, "Read it and pass it on to others." I never realized she was even listening to my words. Barry soon after this was moved to a nice rehab close to my house. I liked this rehab because they were very methodical in their methods of helping him. His family came every week to visit him. His 2 sons came on Sunday and he was in a wheelchair.

A few months later I was in the rehab one day and I was really excited that Barry was starting to walk. I was praising him for every step he took. When the lessons were over we sat down on the couch and just rested. A man sat down beside me on the couch. He said that he had noticed how I praised Barry for his progress. He said it impressed him very much. I listened to him talk and he told me that he believes that there are many Gods. I asked him if I could share a story with him and he said, "Yes" I shared my butterflies story. Then he talked about Buddha and he did not know which one to believe in. I asked him if I could share another story with him. He agreed and I told him about the keyed cars at school and how mine was saved because of my God telling me that I would not be there the next day. I went home and prayed that the man's eyes would be opened to my God. The next morning the man told me he had prayed a prayer for us last night. Thank you, Lord. I want the atheist to believe because if they don't they go to Hell, a place I want none to go to. God will save you if you call out to him and believe that he exists and ask him to come into your life. Then go through the sinner's prayer and believe in your heart that Jesus is your Savior. He will not hesitate. I shared this with my Sunday School and we all prayed for him (that man) to believe. I also shared with my Sunday School my life with my God. A lot of the testimony was what I have put in this book. That testimony in my Sunday School was a precursor of this book. It set me up to write this book. I want everyone to know that they can have a relationship like I do with my Jesus. I had to hunger for him and I found him and he became real to me. He gave his life for me and saved me from my sins.

Barry after 100 days in this rehab went home to my house. We had rehab at my house and they came 2 to 3 times each week. We had a visitor almost every day. He was in a wheelchair and I got him a power chair that would allow him to go almost anywhere. I got ramps for my house and I took out a doublewide jacuzzi and put in a walk - in shower with handrails for Barry. I also got a pedestal sink put in that bathroom. Another thing I did for Barry I paid all his bills for him. I made sure his insurance, electric bill, gas bill, and any other bills he had were paid. I did not want his house electricity cut off because he has beautiful wood floors and freezers dripping water would ruin them. I did not have power of attorney yet and I knew that I had to help him out in every way I could. I had to get his mail delivered to my house and pay them as they came in.

A Sunday after a week I was in my present church worshipping my Lord with all that I am. One of the Sunday School class members had their grand-daughter with them and they were seated several rows back from me. The grand daughter told her grandmother that she loved the passion I showed as I worshipped the Lord. The granddaughter said, "The lady with the long hair worships deeply our God." Her grandmother told me that she had said this about me. I was so happy that she recognized the love I have for my Jesus. I will always love him and adore him in his house.

Barry learned to walk with the help of his occupational therapist. She was so encouraging and I made sure she was praised for her efforts. She reminded me of the nurse in Charlotte that truly had her mind on her patient. He progressed so greatly that we don't use a wheelchair at all and the ramps are gone. This stroke happened on January 25,2016. Barry then had rehab off sight and we had to go to his rehab. He got 2 straps to hold up his shoulder and the right arm. I met a lady in the waiting room and we had a fantastic testimony to each other. She had met the Lord Jesus and he told her she was now ready to serve him. She told me she has been on fire for the Lord since that day. I also told her about my times with the Lord. She was so sweet and we enjoyed sharing our lives.

As I write this book it is the summer of 2017. Barry does not speak except yes and no. He cannot read or answer the phone. His right hand is in a sling and he can walk, bathe himself, use the restroom by himself, and dress himself. I am his caretaker. He and I have Bible studies, pray the Lord's prayer together, and praise the Lord together every day. I go out in my yard and praise the Lord on my ipod. I love being able to care for him and be able to share with others the gospel. We both attend church every Sunday and have Sunday School that we attend also. Barry walks in the church and no use of a wheelchair. God is so good. I also got power of attorney and he paid me back the 7k I paid for the 6 months I paid his bills. He gets money from retirement like me. I take care of his finances and I have made him debt free and we have torn up his credit card. We visit his house every month for repairs and just to visit.

After a visit to rehab to see Barry I went to Walmart and ran into my son's friend's mom that I had not seen in a long time. We talked for over 2 hours and she shared with me and I shared with her. I told her about the butterflies, dad visiting Heaven, 1st grade teachers telling me I was going to have a witch next year, God calling me off my job. The wreck Barry and I had, and my children not in church and hers not in church either. We prayed over our children and for our Lord to come into their lives. We were concerned about our children. Our conversation seemed to turn to their busy lives and how they don't have time for the Bible, or prayer, and a life with Jesus in control. Our desire is for our children to come into a relationship with our Savior.

A few months later a pastor was having a bad time with his congregation. They were sending him ugly letters and not signing their names to those scathing words. So, I sat down and wrote this Pastor a letter to try to build him up for the fight he was facing. In the letter, I told him to fight the Devil and he will flee. Fight for your church. Recognize that greater is He that is in me than he that is in the world. I told him about my life and how it came crashing down when Barry had his stroke. How the Lord took my hand tenderly and led me through that valley. I said, "I found a ministry in the Hospitals and rehabs that I could reach out and be a mouthpiece for my Lord." I said, "From ashes rose up beauty." I reach out to the lost every place I am. Then I told him about the demon that was in my bedroom and how he fled at the name of Jesus. I then praised the pastor and told him that God has him there and he is making a difference. I said, "That church was dead until you arrived and brought the life back into that church." I told him that he was a joy to listen to and this church belongs to him and not Satan. A few weeks later he decided to stay and fight for his church. Praise the Lord for he is mighty; Mighty at bringing down strongholds.

One of the deepest in the Lord couple in my church lost their son and walked with the Lord through this valley and came out on the other side trusting the Lord. I had seen, as a teacher that when a couple loses a child it brings so much sorrow that they cannot seem to rise above the sorrow. I really prayed for this couple to not lose the trust they had with the Lord but would come out trusting the Lord that it was in His hands. They did exactly this and you can tell that they miss him but they believe that they are in God's hands and he will not fail them. I went to the funeral and they were so congenial and trusting it really impressed me that their faith is so great it takes them through the deepest valley and helps them no matter what they face. Jesus is there. Thank you, Lord.

LESSONS ON SUBJECTS THE LORD ASKED ME TO SHARE

A. Forgiveness lessons (by Pastor Steve Brown)

My Sunday School teacher taught about Joseph and the way he was so forgiving to his brothers. I want to share some of his findings and to help you when you face unforgiveness. When Joseph responded to his brother's guilt and fear of retaliation he did two things: he wept before them (demonstrating a tender heart) and then he reassured them of his love and concern (demonstrating that he really cared for them). Joseph was able to respond this way because he had learned how to take his proper place under God. "Am I in God's place?" (50-19). The same is true for us when we're tempted to withhold forgiveness or to seek vengeance. Three things are necessary for us to take our proper place under God.

    1.   We must allow him to be the definitive judge in all things. The Lord says "Vengeance is mine, I will repay." (Rom. 12:19). So, if we really love our neighbor as God expects us to, we must desire his mercy for that person just as much as we want mercy for ourselves.

2. We must humble ourselves under God's rule. If you have a humble attitude toward those who wronged you, you won't bring up the past and you won't remind them how you were right and they were wrong. Instead you lay aside the wrong and then seek to strengthen the relationship.

3. We must believe that God and how He works are always, ultimately good. The NT equivalent of Joseph's word to his brothers is found in Romans 8:28 "And we know that the Lord causes everything to work together for the good of those who are called according to His purposes for them".

Human pride will always endeavor to short circuit forgiveness. Exercising humility is the first and maybe the most important step toward forgiveness. Pride will try to keep us from forgetting what someone did to wrong us. Joseph didn't carry a scorecard and we shouldn't either. Humility forgives and forgets. We must learn to speak the truth in love. (Eph. 4;15). Joseph was frankly honest but kind when he said "You meant to harm me." True forgiveness doesn't deny the offense nor cover it up as if it did not happen. But neither is forgiveness brutal by rubbing it in. For healing to take place the offended person needs to admit his guilt and know that you know what he did. Joseph's brothers needed to hear him agree that they had wronged him. WHY? Because they couldn't be sure he had forgiven them until they were sure that he understood the magnitude of the offense.

Genuine forgiveness will lead to...
Sincerely pray for God's mercy toward that person.
Look for ways to be kind to them.

Make it clear that we want to restore the relationship.

Finally, to forgive others we must, in fact, genuinely care. Joseph's forgiveness proved itself in his kind deeds long after the fact. Just like faith, words are nothing if they aren't backed up by action. A forgiving spirit manifests itself through kind and thoughtful deeds. Forgiveness frees you to experience God's abundant grace and makes you a channel of that grace even toward the one who wronged you.

Mr. Andrew Murray once gave this advice to a lady. He said, "In time of trouble, say, First, he brought me here. It is by his will that I am in this strait....in that I will rest. Next, he will keep me here in his love, and give me grace in this trial to behave as his child. Then, He will make the trial a blessing, teaching me lessons he intends me to learn, and working in me his grace he means to bestow. And Last, in his good time he can bring me out again. How and when, he knows. Therefore, I am here by God's appointment, in his keeping, under his training, for his time."

I have found this is very true in my life. When I went through those 2 valleys (my 2 husbands almost died) I knew I was on a journey and he ordained it for me and I knew I was under his loving care and in his time, it all worked out for the good of the saint who serves him. That saint was me. Try this advice and it truly works and it is the way of life for a Christian.

B. Lessons on Hell

Why is there a Hell?

Prisons are for the ones who break the laws and to protect the innocent. Hell has been prepared for the offenders of God's law. Hell was not prepared for man but for the devil and his angels. (Matt. 25:41). If you want to reject God, then there is a place prepared that has nothing to do with his goodness. Salvation is God's free gift and we must receive it, so we can be saved. God loves you and he wants you to love him. He doesn't want you to go to hell. It will be your own fault if you go there. Don't break God's law. Jesus said, "Unless you repent you will likewise perish." (Luke 13:3, John 3:36, Rom. 10:9-10).

Is God mean for putting people in Hell?

My God doesn't send anyone to hell! He sent Jesus his son to keep us from going to hell. (John 3:16, 6:40, 12:47). Because we are sinners, we cannot live in his perfect Heaven as we are; We have to be born again with our Jesus. When we trust in His son, we become new in Christ and his shed blood for our sins. (Rom. 5:8, 1st John 1:7). Jesus suffered an agonizing death on the cross to keep us out of hell. He loves you, even those who deny him and mock him.

Is the fire real?

Remember the rich man in hell asking Lazarus for a drop of water to cool his tongue as he was tormented by the flame. If it was only mental thoughts or something other than fire, then why would water do the trick? Jesus mentioned hell in 46 verses and 18 of them spoke of the fires of hell. Jerusalem had a city dump called Gehenna and it burned continually. It burned unclaimed dead bodies that were thrown into its fire. My sister once had a vision of a large pit. On the edge of the pit was men and women marching in a line blindly towards the pit. As they got close to the edge they would drop like dominoes into that pit and the one behind them would drop next. Like soldiers they fell into the fires of hell. Don't be one of them, I pray. Find my Jesus and love him and repent of your sins and you will not be one of those people. Heaven is your home and love abounds for you there. I pray I see you in Heaven and we rejoice in the love we have for each other.

I one time saw a man's (teenager) testimony on TV. He was shot and found himself in the back seat of a car. His spirit left his body and went down. He saw the axle on the car as he descended down until he heard cries of anguish and smelt flesh burning in the pits of hell. He was screaming, "NO, NO." Back at home his mother was on her knees praying for her son since she had felt he was in danger. He descended down into the fire and all of a sudden, he was lifted back past the axle of the car and back into his body. His mom's prayers had saved him from the fires of hell and he was eternally thankful, because he became a Man of God and preached the rest of his life. Mom's prayers were powerful. She loved him and prayed him back into his body. Praise the Lord.

C.   Lessons on Gambling and Tithing

Gambling and the Lottery is spiritual suicide. 1st Timothy 6:10 (for the love of money is a root of all kinds of evil for which some have strayed from the faith in their greediness and pierced themselves through with many sorrows). 1st Timothy 6:9 says that those who desire to be rich fall into temptation and a snare, and into many foolish and harmful lusts which drown men in destruction and perdition. It replaces our love of Jesus. All that we have belongs to God. We are stewards of his money. We don't gamble with Master's money. God gives the ability (talents) to work and we work for God.

It is a kind of embezzlement. Look to the men who were given talents to their ability. One was given 5, another 2, and another 1. Remember the one with 5 produced 5 more. The man with 2 made 2 more. The man with 1 buried his. Remember the Master honored the men with 5 and 2 and said, "Well done, good and faithful servants; you were faithful over a few things, I will make you over ruler over many things." To the one who received 1 the Master said, "You wicked and lazy servant." The Master cast the unprofitable servant into outer darkness where there will be weeping and gnashing of teeth. (Matthew 25: 14-30).

Don't embezzle money that is not yours. We will have to give an account of what we did with our money. Gambling is foolish and smart people lose. The House controls that action and those machines. It is all rigged. We become addicted and we love it. Break free and invest your money in God's house. Give him 10% of your gross. He will bless you and money will not matter because he blesses you whereby money takes a back seat in your life. It is the least of your worries.

Malachi 3:8 says Will a man rob God? Yet you rob me. But you ask, "How do we rob you?" In tithes and offerings. You are under a curse -the whole nation of you- because you are robbing me. Bring me the whole tithe into the storehouse, that there may be food in my house. Test me in this, says the Lord Almighty, and see if I will not throw open the floodgates of Heaven and pour out so many blessings that you will not have room enough for it. I will prevent pests from devouring your crops, and the vines in the field will not cast their fruit, says the Lord Almighty.

Jesus once said, "Many Christians are poor and have many problems in their lives because their hearts are not right with me and they will not tithe. Any Christian who doesn't tithe will not be blessed because they love money more than my word." Jesus wants you and I to let him be the caretaker of us. He blesses me with many souls to share him with and that is more important than any money on this earth. My life belongs to him and so does my money. People are my treasure to share my Lord Jesus with them.

Footnotes....

Psalms 91

Now I want to share a few of the things I have searched for and found in the Bible.

This is the promises in Psalms 91 (23 promises).

A. I abide under the shadow of the Almighty.
B. Say, "He is my refuge and my fortress: my God, in him will I trust."
C. Deliver me from the snare of the fowler
D. From the noisome pestilence
E. Cover me with His feathers
F. And under His wings shalt thou trust
G. His truth shall be my shield and buckler
H. Not be afraid of the terror by night nor for the arrows that flieth by day
I. Nor the pestilence that walketh in darkness
J. Nor for the destruction that wasteth at noonday
K. A thousand shall fall at thy side, and ten thousand at thy right hand; but it shall not come nigh thee
L. Only with my eyes shall I behold and see the reward of the wicked

M. No evil shall befall me

N. Neither shall any plague come nigh my dwelling

O. Shall give your angels charge over me, to keep me in all your ways.

P. Shall bear me up in their hands, lest I dash my foot against a stone.

Q. I shall tread upon the lion and the adder; the young lion and dragon shall I trample under my feet

R. Because I have set my love upon thee, therefore I will deliver him

S. I will set him on high because he has known my name.

T. I shall call upon you, and you will answer me

U. You will be with me in trouble.

V. You will deliver him and honor me with long life will I satisfy Him

W. Show me your salvation.

ABC's of Faith

ABC"s of Faith (EPH. 5:1-2)

A. Always give thanks. 1st Thess. 5:16-19

B. Build others up. 1st Thess. 5:11-15

C. Cast your cares on Him. Psalms 55:22

D. Delight in God's word. Jer. 15:16

E. Expect great things. Eph. 3:20

F. Forgive as you have been forgiven. Col. 3:12-14

G. Give cheerfully and generously. 2nd Cor. 9:6-20

H. Humble yourself. 1st Peter 5:5-6

I. Increase your faith. 2nd Peter 1:5-10

J. Joy in the Journey. Phil. 4:11-13

K. Know his Love. Eph. 3:16-19

L. Listen to His wise counsel. Prov. 11:14; 24:6

M. Make peace with others. Matt. 5:22-24

N. Never give up. Gal. 6:9-10

O. Overflow with kindness. Eph.4:31-32

P. Pray without ceasing. Eph. 6:18

Q. Quiet yourself. Psalms 46:10

R. Renew your mind. Romans 12:2

S. Seek to do His will. Matt. 7:17-27

T. Tell the truth in love. Eph. 4:15-16

U. Use the gifts God has given you. Romans 12:4-8

V. Value Godliness. 1st Tim. 4:7-9

W. Work unto the Lord. Col. 3:22-24

X. Experience His presence. 1st Peter 1:8-9

Y. Yield to others. Phil. 2:3-8

Z. Zealously share the reason for your hope. 1st Peter 3:14-16

THE NAMES OF JESUS

This is a list of the names of Jesus off the chart hanging in Barry's home....

and thou shalt call his name....

1. Jesus -Mt. 1:21
2. Prince of Peace- Is. 9:6
3. Mighty God- Is. 9:6
4. Wonderful Counselor- Is. 9:6
5. Holy One- Mk.1:21
6. Lamb of God-- Jn. 1:29
7. Prince of Life- Acts: 3:15
8. Lord God Almighty- Rev. 5:5
9. Lion of the Tribe of Judah- Rev. 5:5
10. Root of David -Rev. 22:16
11. Word of Life- Ist Jn.1:1
12. Author and Finisher of our Faith- Heb. 12:2
13. Advocate- Ist Jn. 2:1
14. The Way- Jn. 14:6
15. Dayspring- Lk. 1:78
16. Lord of All- Acts 10:16
17. I Am- Jn. 8:58

18. Son of God- Jn. 1:34

19. Shepherd and Bishop of Souls- Ist Pet. 2:25

20. Messiah- Jn. 1:41

21. The Truth- Jn. 14:6

22. Savior- 2nd Pet. 2:20

23. Chief Cornerstone- Eph. 2:20

24. Kings of Kings- Rev. 19:16

25. Righteous Judge- 2nd Tim. 4:8

26. Light of the World- Jn. 8:12

27. Head of the Church- Eph. 1:22

28. Morningstar- Rev. 22:16

29. Sun of Righteousness- Mal. 4:2

30. Lord Jesus Christ- Acts 15:14

31. Chief Shepard- 1st Pet. 5;4

32. Resurrection and Life- Jn. 11:25

33. Horn of Salvation and Life- Lk. 1:69

34. Governor- Mat. 2:4

35. The Alpha and the Omega- Rev. 1:8

MY LOVE LETTER

I write Letters to my Lord, and here is a Letter written to the Lord on Good Friday of 2016 while Barry was in rehab.

Dear Lord Jesus (my Savior and my Salvation), Yahweh, my God, the Trinity

I want to write this Letter to you and thank you for the sacrifice that you gave some 2 thousand years ago. You took my sin upon you and it was so evil that you could not look upon it for you are so HOLY. Thank you for the willingness to save me and give me Grace. It is your free gift that you gave me and I love you for all you did. You are not willing that any person should perish. You love us all and you gave your life for ALL mankind. Lord, I pray daily for the unbelievers and somehow a missionary or believer crosses their paths and brings life into them. Have mercy, Lord, and light up their world with the gospel (the good news) that gives them eternal life and Heaven as their home one day. Lord, I love you, worship you, adore you, and think you are so beautiful and lovely in my eyes. I want one day to see you and gaze on you and tell you what you mean to me. One day I will get to be with you. I pray for that day that it is not far away. My heart, soul, spirit, strength, and all that is Beth, bless you and love you and adore you. Lord, The words are hard to come by to truly tell you what you mean to me. I belong to you and I never want to be without you all the days I am left on this earth. Come close, Lord, and may the meditations of my heart and the words of my mouth be pleasing to you. Make me holy, pure, and lovely in your sight. Help me be your mouthpiece every day on this earth. Bring people across my path and give me the words to open their hearts to you, My Jesus. My heart yearns to work for you and be a helpmate to others. Like this week, I took that dogwood bloom to Barry to remind him of our Lord Jesus's sacrifice. As I was telling him, A little nurse wanted to hear it too. So, I told her about the blood points on the dogwood on each corner (the tree you were slain on). All the places that your blood was poured out. Your precious blood poured out of your head, 2 hands, and your feet. They were also the places where you felt the intense pain. Your head, by the thorns, and your feet and hands by those huge nails they pounded into your flesh. I cringe when I hear that because I know it was painful. OH, my Lord Jesus, I love you forever and ever. My love knows no bounds. My love for you is eternal, Lord. Please know how thankful I am for you loving me so much you gave up your life for me. Oh, precious Savior, I love you, you are my king and the ruler of my life. I gave my life to you over 30 years ago and I have never stopped loving you and I never will. Thanks to you for your love that is so deep and sweet.

Loving *you* deeply, sweetly,

Forevermore, in Jesus name,

Beth, a child of God

Lists of mine found on a Bible hunt

I have made up lists that I have researched throughout the Bible about praise and the Holy Spirit……

All who praise our God, Yahweh, Abba, and my Jesus

1. His angels
2. All his Heavenly Host
3. Sun
4. Moon
5. Shining stars
6. Waters above the skies
7. Great sea creatures
8. All ocean depths
9. Lightning
10. Hail
11. Snow
12. Clouds
13. Stormy winds that do his bidding
14. Mountains

15. All hills

16. Fruit trees

17. All cedars

18. Wild animals

19. All cattle

20. Small creatures

21. Flying birds

22. Kings of the earth

23. All nations

24. Princes

25. All rulers on earth

26. Young men

27. Maidens

28. Old men

29. Children

30. All his saints

31. Israel

32. People close to his heart

33. The heavens

34. The heights above

35. All you have made (everything)

What the Holy Spirit does for us....

1. He begets us into the family of God

2. He seals us or marks us as God's

3. He dwells in us

4. He unites us to Christ

5. He changes us into the likeness of Christ

6. He helps us in prayer

7. He comforts

8. He guides

9. He strengthens will power

10. He is the source of power and fruitfulness

How to praise Him, Jesus and Yahweh...

1. Sing to the Lord a new song

2. Praise the Lord

3. His praise in the assembly of Saints

4. Israel rejoices in their maker

5. People of Zion be glad in their King

6. Praise his name with dancing

7. Make music to him with tambourines and harp and dancing

8. Saints rejoice in his honor

9. Sing for joy on their beds

10. May the praise the of God be in their mouths

11. A double- edged sword in their hands

12. He crowns the humble with salvation

13. The Lord takes delight in His people

14. Praise God in His Sanctuary

15. Praise Him in His mighty Heavens

16. Praise Him in His acts of power

17. Praise Him for His surpassing greatness

18. Praise Him with the sounding of the trumpet

19. Praise Him with the strings and the flute

20. Praise Him with the clash of cymbals

21. Let everything that has breath praise the Lord

22. Sing to the Lord with thanksgiving

23. Joyfully sing of your righteousness

24. All you have made will praise you, oh, Lord

25. Let every creature praise His Holy name forever and ever

Reasons for praise…

1. Because of the splendor, glory, majesty, and beauty of our God

2. Our God who created the Heavens and Earth

3. The one who is to be exalted in his Holiness

4. The experience of God's mighty acts, particularly his acts of salvation and redemption; In doing so, we praise God for His unfailing mercy and grace.

5. For God's continual provential care and provision for us day by day, both physically And spiritually.

6. For any specific acts of deliverance in our lives such as being rescued from our Enemies.

David said, "I will praise you, Oh Lord, with all my heart;
I will tell of all your wonders. I will be glad and rejoice in
You; I will sing praise to Your name, Oh Most High.

How to get close to My Jesus

I will share with you about my relationship with my Lord and what I do in my life to allow Him to be so active in my everyday living.

1. I write thank you notes to my God in a spiral notebook. I thank Him for His help and the things He does in my life. Ex. NO. 14- Thank you for the dreams you bring me that helps me understand the future. You are my help in times of need. I love you and adore you and thank you for your hand in my life. (I started with no.1 (numbering the ways he helps me and loves me) and I am now at 1168 as of 2017.)

2. I praise Him with my ipod and my stereo in my home and on a cd player at Barry's house. If outside, I praise the Lord with my ipod and know that the birds and the trees are worshipping with me. God told me this. I also praise him in my home with my cd player and I dance to my God and Worship him in truth and passion.

3.   I read the Bible and scripture to Barry every morning and we pray the Lord's prayer together. We also go on Tuesdays down to my mom or sister's home to have a Bible study with them. We pray together and have a lunch together.

4. I give a 10% tithe to my church and 30$ more to missions. Barry also gives his 10% tithe and 20$ to missions. God requires this amount and I always give for 30 years and more.

5. I write letters of love to my Savior and my God. I declare my love and devotion to him. A copy of my letter is before this list.

6. My magazines are Christian and they are Charisma, Midnight Call, News of Israel, and Angels on Earth.

7. I support Israel and send money to those people in need over there. I also give to needy people that come across my path. God will prompt me when to give and how much.

8. I obey my God when he tells me to do something like call me off my job.

9. I pray for lists I have in my Bible. I have a list of names of family members, friends, unbelievers, our country, the world, people I do not know, Churches, and for the salvation of those who don't know my Jesus.

10. I have scripture cards on my door of my house and other places in my home.

11. I have a living room that has the picture of Jesus the way the children who visited Heaven saw him, the Lord's supper, the 10 command-ments, the plaque that I put up for giving my home to the Lord, and a sign that says "This house believes in Jesus."

12. I strike up a conversation with others no matter where I roam. I love to tell the story of how he works in my life. That is why I want to share this book with all who desire to serve Him.

13. I host Christmas in my home and share every Christmas with my family the scriptures of that special night when our Savior was born. Sometime I share the story of Rapture in a Christmas story. We have a few who don't know my Lord and it is for their sake I share Him. I do not put up a tree but a manger scene …the true meaning of Christmas.

14. I have a faith card I pass out to people who will take it. It is a card that asks the questions about your faith.

15. I pray with people over the phone. If they are sick I offer to pray for healing. It may also be about a new job.

16. I give out over 50 Christmas cards at Christmas and I make sure they honor my Jesus and not just happy holidays.

17. If God has done something in my life that week I share it in my Sunday School class with the group.

18. I meet on Jan. 1st at the parking lot with my God and ask for souls to cross my path and help them to believe.

19. On Feb. 7th I meet the Lord in the back woods behind my house to dedicate my life to him. I sing and worship him and tell him I am His and I will work for Him.

20. I look for crosses in the woods and forests and sometimes they are glowing.

21. I look in the sky for angel formations and any other things the Lord reveals.

22. I lay on my bed and face the 2nd story windows and watch for the clouds to pass by and make formations of angels and other things. I recently requested a heart shaped cloud. I saw it.

23. I talk to my God anyplace at any time and cry out to him when I need help and he always provides.

24. Before I buy anything that I want, I always ask my God to help me find what I need and may it be dependable and worthy to own. After the Lumina van, I learned to ask.

25. I pray every morning that he will fill me with his Grace and lead my life that day and, "good morning" to the Holy Spirit as I look out the window on a new day.

26. I wear a cross around my neck and have worn it for 30 years. I also wear a cross ring on my right hand that I placed there when I gave my life to my Savior around 7 years ago.

27. I have a book shelf that Lee built for me and it houses all the Christian books I have collected over the 30 years I have been a believer. It has 5 shelves and it measures 6 feet by 6 feet. I call it my Christian library.

28. I have a picture of Jesus coming on the clouds with his angels to rapture us. It reminds me of a day that is in our future when He comes for His church.

29. I have a DVD library of Christian films and when there is nothing on tv to watch we plug in one of these.

30. I pray the blood of Jesus over my home and Barry's home and he is the protector of our homes. He loves for us to trust him and know that he is always there.

31. I am on my birthday in 2018 going to Israel with my church. I may have to write another book after that trip. I am going with my good friend. I asked the Lord on the way to the church meeting about the trip that if he wanted me to go he would make everything fall into

place and I would know. I looked around and saw a few people I knew and then my friend entered the meeting; I knew then that I was to go. My face lit up when she entered the room. We agreed to be roommates and enjoy the trip together. Barry will be cared for by some ladies that will come in and be his caregiver for about the price I am paying to go on this trip. I have made arrangements with these caretakers for next year. So, God paved the way for me to go. I will be baptized in the Jordan River by my Pastor just like my Jesus. I will get to visit Bethlehem where my Lord was born on this earth. I will ride in a boat on the Sea of Galilee just as my Savior did. I will get to see the Mount of Olives where my Savior will return. Thank you, Lord Jesus.

32. This past Sunday a sweet lady was in a wheelchair for a long time. I know her and she is always smiling and happy. A man in the congregation was trembling under the power of the Lord and he told her the Lord asked him to pray for her healing. He prayed over her and she got out of the wheelchair and walked. God had super naturally healed that sweet soul right then. She walked out of the church and had never done this before. God can do anything. I will always pray for others and their healing.

33. Trust the Lord with your decisions. I do, and it will turn out better than ever for you. If you go to buy a car ask the Lord to help you pick it out. It will thrill you when you see what he brings you.

34. I pray over people, I pray daily for my Jesus to help me to be His mouthpiece, and I pray for protection everywhere I go. I ask the Lord to protect me in my travels. I pray anywhere and anytime I desire.

He is my constant companion in my life. I pray over churches and ambulances when they come across my path.

About the Author

I am Beth Springer. I was married to Lee Springer one month shy of 33 years. We had 2 children, and the girl is in her 30's and lives in Aiken. My son is almost 30 and he lives 5 minutes away from me. I was a first- grade teacher and I dearly loved teaching. No one could talk me out of quitting my job but my Lord. He spoke on May 6 ,2010, and asked me to stop teaching and I obeyed him. I married my 2nd husband, Barry in 2012. We are still married, and he can walk, but cannot talk except yes and no. He had this stroke in 2016. We visit his house once a month and then back to my house. He owns a house in Rock Hill and my home is in Lexington. I met my Lord on the beach at Edisto in 1992. It is a special beach because I met my Lord there and He sent those butterflies for me to dance with and know He was real. This book tells of my walk with the Lord and how He helps me and protects me every day of my life. I am desiring to help others understand how to walk closer to My God by doing some of the things I do to get close. You must do this with a heart that desires it or your efforts will be futile. Get on fire for our Lord and He will come alive in you. Hunger for Him and He is ready and willing. Here is a sinner's prayer; Pray these words and believe. "Lord Jesus, come into my life and become the master of my soul. Forgive me of my sins. I believe that you died on the cross to save me from my sins. I believe you rose again and you live in Heaven, and I give you me. Help my unbelief and help me to know you as my Savior. In Jesus name, I pray". If you prayed that and you believe in your heart that it is true, then you are saved. Serve him and love him and life for you will be eternal. Heaven is our eternal home and one day we will go there. I hope to see you there. I am not writing these words for gain but because I want these words to touch people and they get to go to Heaven. I want the unbelievers to come into a knowledge of my Lord Jesus. I desire no one to go to that terrible place. I have read Mary Baxter's book about hell and after reading it, I pray deeply for the unbelievers. Read it and it will bring light into your life. God Bless you who reads this book. May it be a light unto your path and bring you eternal life. I am praying for you and your salvation. God Bless you with deep faith. We all have free choice and we decide where we reside after this life on earth. The ticket to Heaven is our Jesus Christ. He died for me and you and has given us a free gift called Grace. If someone asks you how to get to Heaven you need to say the only way to Heaven is believe that Jesus Christ is your Savior. There is no other way to get to Heaven but by the blood of Jesus Christ. He paid the price for me and you and he is just waiting for your response. God be with you, and Jesus be with you as your best friend in the days ahead. I am praying for you and that you will believe.

Lord God in Heaven,

I pray that this person that is before you today make the decision to follow you and be with you in their heart and soul. Come alive in their life and reside as the Holy Spirit inside this person. Have mercy and bring them into your kingdom. I pray they accept the sinner's prayer and ask you to come into their lives. Lord, help them to believe and become your child. I ask this in Jesus name, amen.

When you pray always at the end of your prayer say, "In Jesus Name I pray." He is our Savior and we owe our lives to Him. God bless you with a life with Jesus.

If you forgot the Sinner's prayer here it is;

"Lord Jesus, I ask you to come into my life and become alive for me. I ask you to forgive me of my sins and to wipe my sins away. I want to be your child. Come into my life in a big way and make me love you and become your blessed child. I give myself to you now and forevermore. I believe that God raised you from the dead and you reign on high in Heaven. In Jesus Name, I pray".

See how easy it is to become a believer. Just say that prayer and believe in your heart that He is real and He will make himself known to you. Talk to him, read his book, the Bible, and pray daily to Him in His name. Then, go someplace to worship him and learn about him in a good church. Make sure the Church teaches about the Holy Spirit. You are on your way to a wonderful life with him at the helm. God be with you and come alive in your life. I love you, and pray for you to have nothing but happiness. All the valleys you never have to face alone. He is there. So, happiness can be yours if you ask Him for help through the valley (bad things happen). That is what I call a valley. Jesus be with you now and forever.

I will back up the way of Salvation by giving you the scripture of the Bible called the Roman's Road of Salvation.

Romans 3:23 – for all have sinned and fall short of the glory of God.

Romans 5:8 – but God shows His love for us in that while we were still sinners, Christ died for us.

Romans 6:23 – For the wages of sin is death, but the free gift of God is eternal life in Christ Jesus, our Lord.

Romans 10:9-10 – Because, if you confess with your mouth, that Jesus is Lord and believe in your heart that God raised him from the dead, you will be saved. For with the heart one believes and is justified, and with the mouth one confesses and is saved.

Romans 10:13 – For "everyone who calls on the name of the Lord will be saved".

Now believe and walk with my Jesus and you are on your way to Heaven; a beautiful mansion built by heavenly hands and waiting on you. Also, you get to be with our Savior and talk and walk with him as if it were your own father on earth. I will be looking for you and I pray that we will get to know each other as a sister or brother of Christ. Hallelujah, Praise the Lord!

FURTHER READING

Heaven is so Real by Choo Thomas (awesome book about Heaven, the rapture, and Jesus's personal words to us)

The Blood by Benny Hinn (this book brought power into my life)

Revealing Heaven 1 and 2 by Kat Kerr (these books helped me understand Heaven and what awaits us there)

Peace with God by Billy Graham (this was the first book I read when I got saved)

A Divine Revelation of Hell by Mary K. Baxter (this book will make a believer out of an unbeliever)

A Divine Revelation of Heaven by Mary K Baxter (uplifting book that will make you desire Heaven)

23 Minutes in Hell by Bill Wiese (this is about a Christian visiting the pits of Hell)

The Anointing by Benny Hinn (this is a book that makes you a mature Christian)

90 minutes in Heaven by Don Piper (this man came and gave his testimony at a church in my community and he had visited Heaven)

Power through Prayer by E.M. Bounds (a book about the prayers we send up and how powerful they are)

To Hell and Back by Maurice s. Rawlings M.d. (a book that will frighten you into believing)

Heaven is for Real by Todd Burpo, (a child visits Heaven and sees his little sister), my picture with Jesus is the picture this little boy says looks like the Jesus he saw in Heaven.

Untying God's Hands by Ernest w. Angley, (it is a very good book that tells how unbelief hinders God's hands in our life)

All About Heaven by Randy Peterson (it tells about Heaven and backs up the Bible)

Horrors of Hell and Splendors of Heaven (about both places we can go)

Jesus Talked to me Today by James Stuart Bell (about children and their relationship with Jesus)

Within Heaven's Gates by Rebecca Springer (a beautiful visit to Heaven)

BIBLIOGRAPHY

The Pond by Casey Springer

Sylvester, the Cat by Casey Springer

Forgiveness Lessons by Pastor Steve Brown

CPSIA information can be obtained
at www.ICGtesting.com
Printed in the USA
JSHW080025201122
33484JS00003B/7

9 781545 625415